The Pathway
Into the
Overcomer's
Walk

by
Betty Miller

First Edition Published 1980
Second Printing 1982
Third Printing 1983
Fourth Printing 1984
Fifth Printing 1987
Sixth Printing 1988
Seventh Printing 1989
Eighth Printing 1991
Ninth Printing 1994
Tenth Printing 2003
Print On Demand

The Pathway Into the Overcomer's Walk

ISBN 1-57149-016-7

CHRIST UNLIMITED MINISTRIES, INC.
Pastor R.S. "Bud" Miller - Publisher
P.O. Box 850
Dewey, Arizona 86327

Printed in U.S.A.

Scripture quotations are taken from the King James Version
unless otherwise indicated.

Contents

Preface

Greetings in the name of our Lord Jesus Christ:

I present this book to the body of Christ as the Holy Spirit presented it to me. I challenge you to allow God's Spirit of truth, and the Bible, to test the accuracy of the words within these pages. This book, part of the Overcoming Life Series, is also addressed to all seekers of truth who know not THE CHRIST UNLIMITED, as it would be my privilege to introduce you to Him.

During the early years of the ministry, I struggled to learn how to hear the voice of God. Once, while nervously waiting to speak before a large audience, and not being sure on what subject I should speak, I posed to the Lord in prayer this question: "Lord, what am I going to say to all these people?" In my spirit, I heard Him very clearly reply, "Betty, I was hoping you would not say anything, as I really wanted to speak." Yes, He wants to speak through us, as we yield to His Spirit. Submitting to the Lord and the guidance of the Holy Spirit, I found, was not only possible, but the only way He wants us to minister. **For it is not ye that speak, but the Spirit of your Father which speaketh in you (Matthew 10:20).**

This book is a gift from the Holy Spirit. I take no credit for it. If something within these pages blesses you, enlightens you, brings you closer to the Lord, releases you from fear or bondage, or heals or delivers you, then please lift your voice in praise to the precious Savior of our souls, Jesus Christ our Lord! On the other hand, if you find some of these things difficult to receive, hard to understand, or totally heretical from your viewpoint, would you also look to the Lord and ask Him if it could possibly be the truth? With an open and honest heart, will you ask God to change any pre-conceived ideas, and be free from traditions to receive of Him, His truth? His truth always brings freedom, never bondage. **And ye shall know the truth, and the truth shall make you free (John 8:32).**

In walking with the Lord, I have found we must obey the

things we feel He is speaking to us. In my personal life, I used to be fearful of speaking for the Lord because I was so afraid of missing Him and making mistakes. (He, of course, has now delivered me of all my fears. Praise Him!) He encouraged me not to quit because of mistakes when He spoke these words to me: "Betty, if I receive the glory and praise for all the things that are a blessing to people, I also receive the responsibility for your mistakes, as long as you are striving to please me. I am able to make even those work for your good." **And we know that all things work together for good to them that love God, to them who are the called according to his purpose (Romans 8:28).** We serve a wonderful, loving God, who encourages us to follow and obey Him that we might be blessed, and in turn bless others!

This book was written as an act of obedience to the Lord, whom I dearly love. I consider it an honor to write for Him. Years ago, when I was in prayer, the Lord spoke that I was to write a book, but I never felt it was God's timing, nor did I feel the unction or anointing to begin this work until now. Over the past year God has performed a series of miracles to confirm that it is now His time, and has made the arrangements for this to become a reality.

I pray that this book, along with the Overcoming Life Series, may help you learn to walk closer to our Lord, as He is THE CHRIST UNLIMITED!

I am, by His love,
A handmaiden of the Lord,

Betty Miller
February, 1980

If any man will do his will, he shall know of the doctrine, whether it be of God, or whether I speak of myself (John 7:17).

Foreword

It just seemed natural that I would do the foreword on this book since my wife, Betty, and myself, are "one flesh." God, through the Holy Spirit, has given by revelation to Betty many truths of His Word, which have been set forth in this book.

The Lord spoke to Betty about ten years ago that she was to write a book for Him, and that He would arrange the right time and place to write it. Betty simply took this vision and set it aside until God began to "quicken" her spirit to bring it forth. One morning, very early, Betty awakened, and began to write as the Lord dictated to her. In giving her this small initial portion of the book, he showed her how, by submitting to His Spirit, and completely yielding to Him, He would feed to her the message He wanted to share with the body of Christ. He also revealed how quickly and easily it would be completed. The messages that God has given in this Overcoming Life Series are to all who desire to become "overcomers" and be "conformed to the image of His son" (**Romans 8:29**). Our Lord is not satisfied that a person remains a "babe" in Christ, but longs for each "babe" to grow to maturity. He desires that we should strive to become overcomers, live the overcoming life, and claim the promises of the inheritance of all things that are to be given to the overcomers.

I thank God that He has allowed me to share such close love and companionship with Betty. I know that within her heart she has no personal ambitions, no personal ends to achieve. Betty has simply been doing the will of the Father in the writing of this anointed book. May the Lord bless you with this book, as He has blessed us in being a part of His work.

Yours in Christ,

Pastor R.S. (Bud) Miller

He that overcometh shall inherit all things; and I will be his God and he shall be my son (Revelation 21:7).

Credits & Acknowledgments

ALL PRAISE AND CREDIT
GOES TO **THE CHRIST UNLIMITED!**

Truly Christ, the Father, and the Holy Spirit, are to be praised, not only for this book, but for our very lives. His sacrifice on Calvary made it possible to know Him and all the members of God's family.

As with the printing of any book, there are lots of people responsible for the words on these pages, physical words as well as spiritual words. All the people that have ever been a part of my life, all the people that have prayed and supported this ministry, my friends and my family have truly contributed to this work. Special credit should be given to my husband, Bud, whose faithful and loving prayers, encouragement, leadership, and love are a big part of this book. Also, to everyone whose books and articles I've read, to the ministers of the Gospel, whose sermons I've heard, I express my gratitude. For each has contributed, in some measure, to this book. The list is endless, but eternity has the records. So instead of naming individuals on this page and giving them earthly credit, I prefer the Lord Jesus Christ to reward them each as only He can. God bless you all, and may you be surprised as you open up the box that contains your heavenly treasures.

For the Son of man shall come in the glory of his Father with his angels; and then he shall reward every man according to his works (Matthew 16:27).

Introduction

THE PATHWAY INTO THE OVERCOMER'S WALK deals with several thorny theological issues that eventually will need to be addressed as believers continue in the pathway of an overcomer. Overcomers are encouraged to take a teachable attitude before the Lord, being willing to have our previous teachings corrected if the Word of God brings us into new light on certain controversial subjects.

This book looks at some of these subjects such as "Can a Christian lose his salvation?" and "What is the sin of blaspheming the Holy Spirit?" We are challenged as overcomers to look to the Holy Spirit as our teacher and prove all our theology by the Word of God and not just accept the teachings of men whom we admire or respect.

THE PATHWAY INTO THE OVERCOMER'S WALK also looks at what the overcomer's rewards will be and encourages all to press on toward the prize of the high calling in Christ Jesus.

The Pathway Into
the Overcomer's Walk

Revelation 21:7: He that overcometh shall inherit all things; and I will be his God, and he shall be my son.

Entering the High Calling

Jesus was the first Son to inherit all things of God and He showed us the way so that we too can come into full maturity and perfection. The path of the overcomer is the same path Jesus walked while He was on this earth, the way of sacrifice and obedience. If we are to rule and reign with the Lord, then we must also suffer with Him. **If we suffer, we shall also reign with him (2 Timothy 2:12).** This does not mean that we will go through exactly the same things Jesus did, nor do exactly the same things He did, but we will be willing to suffer the loss of all things here and lay down our lives for the Lord. The things of this earth will not matter, as those who desire to inherit all things in the Lord will have heavenly vision.

The steps that Jesus took were obedient steps. He accomplished the will of the Father. The Lord has a plan for each Christian so that he too might do the perfect will of the Father. If we desire, we can know and walk in that plan. All Christians will not reach the ultimate intention for which they are born. However, it is the Lord's will for all to enter into His high calling if they so choose. **For whom he did foreknow, he also did predestinate to be conformed to the image of his Son, that he might be the firstborn among many brethren (Romans 8:29).** What Paul is saying here is that God decided beforehand or planned ahead a

1

way for us to be conformed to His image. This is the meaning of predestination. God's predestined purpose for all of His sons is to be like Jesus, although many will miss the mark of the high calling of God.

Paul pressed forward to the place of the overcomer and finally attained it as we see from the next two Scriptures.

I press toward the mark for the prize of the high calling of God in Christ Jesus. Let us therefore, as many as be perfect, be thus minded (Philippians 3:14-15). I have fought a good fight, I have finished my course, I have kept the faith: Henceforth there is laid up for me a crown of righteousness, which the Lord, the righteous judge, shall give me at that day: and not to me only, but unto all them also that love his appearing (2 Timothy 4:7-8).

Those, like Paul, who learn to rule and reign in their own lives here on earth by overcoming all that is carnal and against God's will, will ultimately rule and reign with God in His kingdom.

Our Goal: Perfection

This is not an impossible task, for many saints throughout the Bible overcame their fleshly weaknesses and evil natures to attain this "perfection." Even David, who committed adultery and murder, overcame and was called "perfect" by God. **For it came to pass, when Solomon was old, that his wives turned away his heart after other gods: and his heart was not perfect with the Lord his God, as was the heart of David his father (1 Kings 11:4).** God looks on hearts, and if we are desiring His will, He will make us strong and enable us to overcome. **For the eyes of the Lord run to and fro throughout the whole earth, to shew himself strong in the behalf of them whose heart is perfect toward him... (2 Chronicles 16:9).**

The requirement for coming into the place of an overcomer

in Christ is the overwhelming desire to do the will of God. The Holy Spirit then empowers weak men and women to rise above the things of this earth and to enter into His rest. In this section, we cannot possibly cover all of the overcomer's walk, but we can begin. We do not have to be a perfected overcomer to enter into heaven, but if we are to rule and reign with Christ, being an overcomer is a requirement.

There are different levels in the kingdom of God. Some will enjoy greater rewards than others according to what they have done on earth. Of course, all will enjoy the bliss and blessings of heaven, but not all will enter into "throneship." If we are desirous of attaining this place in Christ, we will steadfastly resist all sin in our lives. We will not want to do anything to offend the Father. This being the case, the devil comes against potential overcomers in a different way.

If he cannot get us to deliberately sin against God, he then attempts to get us to push a truth too far. Thus we still commit an abomination to the Lord as **Proverbs 11:1** says, **A false balance is abomination to the Lord: but a just weight is his delight.** Let us look at some truths that are commonly pushed to one extreme or the other, creating imbalance in our spiritual walk. If we are aware of these, then we can avoid them.

Freedom Includes Responsibility

One of these truths is the blessing of Christian freedom. However, if this is abused it results in undisciplined Christians. In Jesus, we have great freedom and liberty. We are not to be under bondage to men's rules and the letter of the law. **Galatians 5:1** says, **Stand fast therefore in the liberty wherewith Christ hath made us free, and be not entangled again with the yoke of bondage.** But we are not to use our freedom as a license to sin.

For, brethren, ye have been called unto liberty; only use not liberty for an occasion to the flesh, but by love serve one

3

another. **For all the law is fulfilled in one word, even in this; Thou shalt love thy neighbor as thyself (Galatians 5:13-14).**

In Christ we have kingly privileges; however, we are always to use them with a servant's heart.

In Satan's kingdom, power is used to exercise a tyrannical chain of dominion over others. The "greater" in his kingdom continue to devour those that are the "lesser" and use them as their servants. This is not so in God's kingdom. The only way to gain authority in His Kingdom is to be a servant.

But Jesus called them unto him, and said, Ye know that the princes of the Gentiles exercise dominion over them, and they that are great exercise authority upon them. But it shall not be so among you: but whosoever will be great among you, let him be your minister; And whosoever will be chief among you, let him be your servant: Even as the Son of man came not to be ministered unto, but to minister, and to give his life a ransom for many (Matthew 20:25-28).

Here again, we must have a proper balance, for at times we shall be a master even as Jesus was, and at other times a servant as He was. **For he that is called in the Lord, being a servant, is the Lord's freeman: likewise also he that is called, being free, is Christ's servant. Ye are bought with a price; be not ye the servants of men. Brethren, let every man, wherein he is called, therein abide with God (1 Corinthians 7:22-24).**

One of the most beautiful examples of the Lord Jesus in the role of servant is the account of his appearance on the seashore after His resurrection. Here is our Lord in His glorified body after winning His greatest victory over the devil, and what do we find Him doing? He is cooking breakfast for His disciples **(John 21)**! He calls them to "come and dine."

We should be good servants for the Lord and reach out to minister to others as He has set forth the example. Not only should we be servants to members of the body of Christ, but in our secular jobs we should also perform our duties with a servant's heart. We should do the best job we can and be a good witness to our bosses. Those who do not have Christian employers sometimes encounter unfair treatment and endure situations that are difficult. However, this is an opportunity to be a good witness for the Lord by bearing patiently with the boss until our prayers effect a change in him. The Lord desires to use the situation to bring redemption not only to the boss, but also to other workmates. We are to do our work unto the Lord, not unto our bosses. God takes note of the job we do and in due time will either promote us or move us if the people around us refuse to respond to the love of Jesus. He has been known to soften even the hardest employer's heart to give raises to those who are pleasing God.

Servants, be obedient to them that are your masters according to the flesh, with fear and trembling, in singleness of your heart, as unto Christ; Not with eyeservice, as men-pleasers; but as the servants of Christ, doing the will of God from the heart; With good will doing service, as to the Lord, and not to men: Knowing that whatsoever good thing any man doeth, the same shall he receive of the Lord, whether he be bond or free (Ephesians 6:5-8).

We must also be careful to give the boss his "money's worth." Many Charismatics get out of balance and witness, fellowship and read on the boss's time. This is acceptable only if our work is caught up and we have permission to do so. To violate this is not a good witness to anyone. People will be more impressed by a job well done than by all our talking about Jesus.

This should also apply to employees who have Christian bosses. Many times they take advantage of the kindness and goodness of their Spirit-filled bosses by coming late to work, taking off frequently, talking and sharing about the Lord while work is neglected. Many feel justified in their laxity, constantly excusing their tardiness because they have been ministering or witnessing to others. We should do our witnessing and studying on our breaks, lunch time, or after hours, not on our boss's time. The Lord will not lead us to minister to others while leaving work undone. Of course, there are times when people have emergency needs, but this is the exception, not the rule. Christians should make excellent workers because their disciplined lives should reflect in their jobs.

The Lord also gave rules for those in places of authority. Christian bosses should abide by the Word of the Lord in dealing with their employees. **And, ye masters, do the same things unto them, forbearing threatening: knowing that your Master also is in heaven; neither is there respect of persons with him (Ephesians 6:9)**. Bosses are to treat their employees as they would desire to be treated themselves, remembering how they would like the Lord to deal with them as their boss. If we would not want to be treated unfairly and to be threatened, then we should not treat our employees that way. The main thing for masters and servants to remember is that they need one another. Therefore, they should seek the Lord if a problem arises, and He will show them how to solve it with fairness to both parties.

In love we should serve one another. We should be flexible so the Lord can mold us through our situations. We should be balanced so that we walk in Christian freedom and extend it to others. But, we must never excuse our lack of self-discipline in the name of Christian freedom. Actually, nothing is clearer in Scripture (and also experience) than the truth that man is free--and responsible. Man chooses without interference or intimidation from God, yet he is left with the responsibility of his choices. Undisciplined lives create situations that need not exist. We must not abuse our freedom; there is always a price to pay should we do so.

Man's Responsibility in Salvation

This truth is clearly demonstrated in the area of our salvation. Man has great difficulty keeping this area in balance mainly because he does not understand the difference between "initial salvation" and "completed salvation." Problems arise when man does not know what part he plays in salvation and what part God plays. Let us examine this issue and discuss God's sovereignty versus man's responsibility in regard to salvation. **...work out your own salavation with fear and trembling (Philippians 2:12). And fear not them which kill the body, but are not able to kill the soul: but rather fear him which is able to destroy both soul and body in hell (Matthew 10:28).**

Some people refuse to take any responsibility for working out their salvation. They claim they are leaving it all to God, and that He will arrange all things that will get them to heaven, even if He has to "drag" them there. He will take away the sin from their lives when He is ready for it to go. They claim it really does not matter what they do. They believe in eternal security to the point that they can never fall away.

The other extreme is salvation by works. If one does good works and is pleasing to God, he can reach heaven; otherwise, he loses his salvation each time he sins. Man either tries to assume all the responsibility for reaching heaven or leaves all the responsibility to God. What does God's Word say about the plan of salvation?

In searching the Scriptures, we find that man must accept God's plan for salvation and not attempt his own. Salvation is a gift and man must come believing in Christ Jesus as the only begotten Son of God who died for his sins.

For God so loved the world, that he gave his only begotten son, that whosoever believeth in him should not perish, but have everlasting life (John 3:16). For the wages of sin is death; but the gift of God is eternal life through Jesus Christ our Lord (Romans 6:23). In accepting this, man then must repent and receive Christ as Lord of his life. Those who desire Christ and walk in His way should never fear losing their salvation as the Lord has promised never to leave them nor forsake them. **Let your conversation be without covetousness; and be content with such things as ye have: for he hath said, I will never leave thee, nor forsake thee (Hebrews 13:5).** However, those

7

who have known the goodness of God and then despise those precious gifts can eventually lose that which they once had.

For if after they have escaped the pollutions of the world through the knowledge of the Lord and Saviour Jesus Christ, they are again entangled therein, and overcome, the latter end is worse with them than the beginning. For it had been better for them not to have known the way of righteousness, than, after they have known it, to turn from the holy commandment delivered unto them (2 Peter 2:20-21).

Nevertheless I have somewhat against thee, because thou hast left thy first love. Remember therefore from whence thou art fallen, and repent, and do the first works; or else I will come unto thee quickly, and will remove thy candlestick out of his place, except thou repent (Revelation 2:4-5).

Since this is a very controversial issue, we need to look at God's Word to establish what He says about eternal security.

The Believer's Security

Coming from a background that taught eternal security to the degree that "once you are saved, you are always saved," I am very well versed in all the Scripture that supports this view. However, when I came into the Spirit-filled walk, I began to study and read opposite views on this subject and came to embrace them. However, I could not find a peace in the extreme of needing to be saved again every time I sinned as that certainly had no security in God's keeping power. Both extremes cause problems in the body of Christ. Let us look to God's Word and find the balance between these two extremes.

God does not want us to take our salvation lightly, nor does He want us to be constantly insecure with the fear of losing our salvation. Therefore, He gives us Scripture to prevent both of these extremes. First, let us look at Jesus' words in **John 10:27-28, My sheep hear my voice, and I know them, and they fol-**

8

low me: **And I give unto them eternal life; and they shall never perish, neither shall any man pluck them out of my hand.** At first glance this Scripture does seem to guarantee an immunity against spiritual loss. However, if we notice the condition for this promise, we will see that it is only those sheep that are listening to and following the Lord that can't be plucked away from the Lord's hand. If they choose to, they may jump out of His hand at any time.

Nowhere in Scripture does God even hint that He will violate the freedom of choice of His followers.

Christians can choose to be lost just as surely as sinners can choose to be saved. When we are "born again" we do not lose our power of choice, for God never overrides the will of man as long as he lives. The Lord desires that all grow in Him to become overcomers, ruling and reigning; yet He does not force anyone to make this choice, even if they are a child of His. Freedom is one of the most beautiful gifts He gives to man. The Lord will bring His people along only as far as they are willing.

There are many Scriptures that show plainly that if a person is not willing to continue to follow the Lord, he can lose the gift God gave him. Just think how useless all the hundreds of Biblical warnings of apostasy would be if it were impossible to fall away. If this could not happen, the Holy Spirit never would have led Peter, Paul and others to pen such solemn admonitions against eternal loss.

The parable of the sower and the seed is a perfect example of those who believe for awhile, but fall away in times of temptation. **Those by the way side are they that hear; then cometh the devil, and taketh away the word out of their hearts, lest they should believe and be saved. They on the rock are they, which, when they hear, receive the word with joy; and these have not root, which for a while believe, and in time of temptation fall away (Luke 8:12-13).** These people had believed, but they fell away. **Now the just shall live by faith: but if any man draw back, my soul shall have no pleasure in him. But we are**

9

not of them who draw back unto perdition; but of them that believe to the saving of the soul (Hebrews 10:38-39). Some do cast away their faith and draw back ending up in perdition (hell).

To those of us who love God, it is very difficult to understand how anyone could desire to leave the Lord and turn back to the world. Nevertheless, it does happen because the Word declares that some will do this. For example, those who have never committed the sin of homosexuality cannot understand how anyone could have this kind of desire, but the Bible speaks of this evil being real, too. The Lord is the only one that can set people free from this demonic influence.

We may not understand how eternal life can be terminated if it is eternal. Certainly eternal life is eternal, but the Bible declares that eternal life cannot be possessed by men apart from a living union with Christ.

And this is the record, that God hath given to us eternal life, and this life is in his Son. He that hath the Son hath life; and he that hath not the Son of God hath not life (1 John 5:11-12).

I am the true vine, and my Father is the husbandman. Every branch in me that beareth not fruit he taketh away: and every branch that beareth fruit, he purgeth it, that it may bring forth more fruit. Now ye are clean through the word which I have spoken unto you. Abide in me, and I in you. As the branch cannot bear fruit of itself, except it abide in the vine; no more can ye, except ye abide in me. I am the vine, ye are the branches: He that abideth in me, and I in him, the same bringeth forth much fruit: for without me ye can do nothing. If a man abide not in me, he is cast forth as a branch, and is withered; and men gather them, and cast them into the fire, and they are burned (John 15:1-6).

Well; because of unbelief they were broken off, and thou standest by faith. Be not highminded, but fear: For if God spared not the natural branches, take heed lest he also spare not thee. Behold therefore the goodness and severity of God:

on them which fell, severity; but toward thee, goodness, if thou continue in his goodness: otherwise thou also shalt be cut off. And they also, if they abide not still in unbelief, shall be graffed in: for God is able to graff them in again (Romans 11:20-23).

We can see that we must keep our faith in God to maintain our union with Him. We have no life apart from our union with Him.

Losing our salvation or falling from grace is not an instantaneous occurrence. It takes time for a branch to wither. We need not fear that if our flesh is weak and we sin we shall instantly lose our salvation. It is difficult for a person to lose his salvation because the Holy Spirit will do all He can to draw that one back to Himself. He will inspire others to pray and will do all within His goodness, mercy and grace to influence the straying one to return. However, if man does not respond to His goodness, then severity falls as the judgment of God is automatic against all sin. God loves the sinner, but hates and judges the sin. If the sinner refuses to part with his sin, then he comes under judgment because of his own choice not to follow God.

God does not want anyone to suffer destruction. But if one chooses that path, He will not prevent it. **If any man defile the temple of God, him shall God destroy; for the temple of God is holy, which temple ye are (1 Corinthians 3:17). If we suffer, we shall also reign with him; if we deny him, he also will deny us (2 Timothy 2:12).** Man can walk in rebellion for a season without losing his salvation. But if he continues, eventually he will cross a line where he no longer has the life of Christ in him. This does not mean that he will be totally lost forever, for he can repent and come back to the Lord at any time before death.

The Unpardonable Sin

The only time that one cannot return to the Lord is when he

has committed the "unpardonable sin." What is this sin? It is a sin the Bible calls the "sin unto death." **If any man see his brother sin a sin which is not unto death, he shall ask, and he shall give him life for them that sin not unto death. There is a sin unto death: I do not say that he shall pray for it (1 John 5:16).** To understand the "sin unto death," we need to look at some other Scriptures.

Jesus clarifies this in **Matthew 12:31-32,**

Wherefore I say unto you, All manner of sin and blasphemy shall be forgiven unto men: but the blasphemy against the Holy Ghost shall not be forgiven unto men. And whosoever speaketh a word against the Son of man, it shall be forgiven him: but whosoever speaketh against the Holy Ghost, it shall not be forgiven him, neither in this world, neither in the world to come.

From this Scripture we can see that the unpardonable sin is blaspheming the Holy Ghost. Since the third person of the trinity is the power and presence of God, one would have to experience this power and presence to blaspheme against Him. The Lord states that He forgives all manner of sin, even blaspheming Jesus, because in His present state of humiliation there might be some misunderstanding of who He really is. But this would not be true concerning the Holy Spirit since anyone with evidence of the Holy Spirit's power who would declare it to be satanic would be exhibiting a condition of heart beyond divine illumination, and therefore would be hopeless.

This is also spoken of in **Hebrews 6:4-6, For it is impossible for those who were once enlightened, and have tasted of the heavenly gift, and were made partakers of the Holy Ghost, And have tasted the good word of God, and the powers of the world to come, If they shall fall away, to renew them again unto repentance; seeing they crucify to themselves the Son of God afresh, and put him to an open shame.**

This kind of sin is not a sin that is committed due to deception or because of some weakness of the flesh. This sin is commit-

12

ted only by someone who is fully enlightened and who at one time has been filled with the Holy Ghost, who knows the Word of God and has experienced the power of the Holy Spirit. If someone turns against God at this point, there is no redemption left for him. **For if we sin willfully after that we have received the knowledge of the truth, there remaineth no more sacrifice for sins (Hebrews 10:26).** It would be like deliberately crucifying the Lord again. This sin results in spiritual death with no forgiveness.

Satan torments many weak Christians with the fear that they have committed the unpardonable sin, making them feel like they can never return to the Lord. If a person has truly committed this sin, he would not even have the desire to return to the Lord. Satan would have completely entered into his heart. Another worry many Christians have is that perhaps their loved ones have strayed too far to be saved. As long as Christians have a burden for someone, there is hope for that person. They would not even carry a burden if there was no hope for the individual, as this would be a sin unto death, and we are instructed not to pray for this sin.

When someone has committed the unpardonable sin, Satan will have been formed in that person's heart and life. Of course, this is not the only sin that will send one to hell. The sin of rejecting Christ as Saviour will also cause one to end up in hell. All men are born in sin and have absolutely no choice about the kind of nature they possess at birth, but the Lord gives us a choice about changing that sinful nature. If we so choose, we can retain that sinful nature and die eternally, or we can receive a new nature through faith in Christ and live eternally.

How can we be assured that we will go to heaven so that Satan does not torment us about losing our salvation? The Bible says if we believe in Christ, we shall have eternal life. The Greek word for "believe" does not mean just a mental assent of accepting Christ, but rather means "to trust in," "to cling to," and "to rely on." If we are trusting in Jesus and relying on Him, then we will have no need to fear the loss of our salvation. **1 John 5:13** says, **These things have I written unto you that believe on the name of the Son of God; that ye may know that ye have eternal life, and that ye may believe on the name of the Son of God.** The Lord wants us to know our future is secure as long as we have faith and follow Him. God's sovereignty is unshakable and His promises are true.

Blessed be the God and Father of our Lord Jesus Christ, which according to his abundant mercy hath begotten us again unto a lively hope by the resurrection of Jesus Christ from the dead, To an inheritance incorruptible, and undefiled, and that fadeth not away, reserved in heaven for you, Who are kept by the power of God through faith unto salvation ready to be revealed in the last time (1 Peter 1:3-5).

From this verse, we can see that we are kept by faith in Jesus. Our faith is what brings us to heaven.

Satan's Target Is Our Faith

Satan is continually trying to destroy our faith by sending every kind of temptation and problem to hinder our walk with God. His target is not really our families, our finances, or our health; it is our faith. He knows if he can destroy our faith in the Lord, he can lead us to hell. **Now the just shall live by faith: but if any man draw back, my soul shall have no pleasure in him. But we are not of them who draw back unto perdition; but of them that believe to the saving of the soul (Hebrews 10:38-39). ...for whatsoever is not of faith is sin (Romans 14:23). But without faith it is impossible to please him: for he that cometh to God must believe that he is, and that he is a rewarder of them that diligently seek him (Hebrews 11:6).**

The goal of our faith is our salvation and this is what is meant by the Scriptures in **Philippians 2:12, ...work out your own salvation with fear and trembling,** and in **1 Peter 1:6-9, Wherein ye greatly rejoice, though now for a season, if need be, ye are** in heaviness through manifold temptations: That the trial of your faith, being much more precious than of gold that perisheth, though it be tried with fire, might be found unto praise and honour and glory at the appearing of Jesus Christ: Whom having not seen, ye love; in whom, though now ye see him not, yet believing, ye rejoice with joy unspeakable and full of glory: Receiving the end of your faith, even the salvation of your souls.

If we desire to be kept by God, then no man can snatch us from the hand of God. God will keep us as long as we desire to be kept and as long as we follow Him in obedience. Disobedience reveals our lack of trust and faith in Christ.

If ye keep my commandments, ye shall abide in my love; even as I have kept my Father's commandments, and abide in his love (John 15:10). Now unto him that is able to keep you from falling, and to present you faultless before the presence of his glory with exceeding joy (Jude 24).

Born of God

Not only can we know that we are going to heaven, but we can reach a place in Christ where more of Christ is formed in us than the world, and therefore it would be impossible for us to fall away. When we become an overcomer in this world, the nature of Christ will be so completely formed in us that we shall no longer have any desires but those of the heavenly Father. We shall only want to do His will, for we will have been conformed to His will; therefore we would have no desire to leave our Father. At this point, one is "born of God."

For whom did he foreknow, he also did predestinate to be conformed to the image of his Son, that he might be the firstborn among many brethren. Moreover whom he did predestinate, them he also called: and whom he called, them he also justified: and whom he justified, them he also glorified

(Romans 8:29-30). **According as he hath chosen us in him before the foundation of the world, that we should be holy and without blame before him in love (Ephesians 1:4). And hath raised us up together, and made us sit together in heavenly places in Christ Jesus. For by grace are ye saved through faith; and that not of yourselves: it is the gift of God: Not of works, lest any man should boast. For we are his workmanship, created in Christ Jesus unto good works, which God hath before ordained that we should walk in them (Ephesians 2:6, 8-10).**

We will either walk with the Lord and continue to have more of His nature formed in us, or we will walk with the devil and continue to have more of his nature. The choice is ours.

When we come to the place where we are truly "born of God," and not just "born again," we shall cease sinning and will keep ourselves from the wicked one. We will have come into the place of maturity and perfection (born into Fatherhood). **He that committeth sin is of the devil; for the devil sinneth from the beginning. For this purpose the Son of God was manifested, that he might destroy the works of the devil. Whosoever is born of God doth not commit sin; for his seed remaineth in him: and he cannot sin, because he is born of God (1 John 3:8-9).**

Paul became an overcomer and had ceased sinning as we find he instructed others to follow him as he followed Christ.

Brethren, be followers together of me, and mark them which walk so as ye have us for an ensample (Philippians 3:17). For though ye have ten thousand instructors in Christ, yet have ye not many fathers: for in Christ Jesus I have begotten you through the gospel. Wherefore I beseech you, be ye followers of me (1 Corinthians 4:15-16). Be ye followers of me, even as I also am of Christ (1 Corinthians 11:1).

Paul had become an overcomer who now walked in "fatherhood." He was fully mature and perfected in Christ and by implication we can know that he no longer sinned or he could not have

16

told others to follow him. Paul still had the sin nature but it no longer controlled him. He ruled over it through the Christ nature that had been formed in him. **But whoso keepeth his word, in him verily is the love of God perfected: hereby know we that we are in him. He that saith he abideth in him ought himself also so to walk, even as he walked (1 John 2:5-6).**

We can behold someone's life and tell whether the Lord is being manifested or Satan is being manifested. **In this the children of God are manifest, and the children of the devil: whosoever doeth not righteousness is not of God, neither he that loveth not his brother (1 John 3:10).** We too can come to the place that Paul attained if we follow in the steps of Jesus.

Follow Christ's Steps

Some of us have not been taught that we can attain our great and high calling in Christ, even though the Word of God tells us that we can. **For even hereunto were ye called: because Christ also suffered for us, leaving us an example, that ye should follow his steps: Who did no sin, neither was guile found in his mouth (1 Peter 2:21-22).** We can have His divine nature manifested in us if we are willing to walk the path that He walked and overcome all sin.

The disciple is not above his master: but every one that is perfect shall be as his master (Luke 6:40). We can see from this Scripture that the Lord desires for us to be perfect and become like Him. **Be ye therefore perfect, even as your Father which is in heaven is perfect (Matthew 5:48).** The Lord would not give us an impossible goal to attain if it were not within our reach to achieve it. We are to be overcomers in all things and not only walk in the ways of our Lord, but also become like Him.

How can we attain this seemingly impossible goal? **But whoso keepeth his word, in him verily is the love of God perfected: hereby know we that we are in him. He that saith he** abideth in him ought himself also so to walk, even as he walked" (1 John 2:5-6).

The Scripture could not be any clearer about God's desire for our lives. However, only those who are willing to walk in His steps will become overcomers. These instructions were not given to man to achieve in the distant future of heaven, but for here and now. Some will utterly disapprove of men becoming like Jesus as they will say it is blasphemous to think men can become Godlike. They disapproved of the same thing in Jesus' day when He said that He was the Son of God. **The Jews answered him, We have a law, and by our law he ought to die, because he made himself the Son of God (John 19:7).** Today, when perfection is taught so that man can rise above the things of this earth and put on those things that are virtuous and glorious, we find men objecting again in spite of what the Word of God says. This is not a cultic teaching saying we are to become gods, but rather we are to become like our God, sons of God who look like their Father.

According as his divine power hath given unto us all things that pertain unto life and godliness, through the knowledge of him that hath called us to glory and virtue: Whereby are given unto us exceeding great and precious promises: that by these ye might be partakers of the divine nature, having escaped the corruption that is in the world through lust. And beside this, giving all diligence, add to your faith virtue; and to virtue knowledge; And to knowledge temperance; and to temperance patience; and to patience godliness; And to godliness brotherly kindness; and to brotherly kindness charity. For if these things be in you, and abound, they make you that ye shall neither be barren nor unfruitful in the knowledge of our Lord Jesus Christ. But he that lacketh these things is blind, and cannot see afar off, and hath forgotten that he was purged from his old sins. Wherefore the rather, brethren, give diligence to make your calling and election sure: for if ye do these things, ye shall never fall (2 Peter 1:3-10).

We can be sure that we shall never fall if we do the above

mentioned things. If we have the divine nature manifested in us, then we shall never fall.

Making Sure of Our Salvation

However, until we reach that place we need to give diligence to making our salvation sure. When we become overcomers we will never need to fear the Lord blotting our name out of His book of life.

He that overcometh, the same shall be clothed in white raiment; and I will not blot out his name out of the book of life, but I will confess his name before my Father, and before his angels. He that hath an ear, let him hear what the Spirit saith unto the churches (Revelation 3:5-6).

If we have spiritual ears we shall hear the Holy Spirit speaking to us to press on and "make our calling and election sure." We can lose that which we have been given if we do not nurture it and yield to the Holy Spirit so that it might grow.

One argument for "once saved, always saved" is based on the analogy of sonship. The reasoning goes, "My child is born into my family and he will always be my child. He cannot be unborn. Whether obedient or disobedient, he will always be my child." This line of reasoning avoids the central issue. The question is not whether a child can be "unborn," but whether it can become sick and die. In fact, if the baby is not fed it will soon die. Unless the Christian lives by the Word of God, he cannot continue to partake of the spiritual life derived through the Holy Spirit.

To disconnect salvation from obedience and its resultant spiritual growth goes against the Word of God. To focus eternal life on a past moment when one once made a decision for Christ is not consistent with the Scriptures. This would eliminate man's free will from that point on, which the Lord never does. We can obey or disobey subsequent revelations of truth, and as we do this, it will undoubtedly effect our final destiny. Willful sin shatters the relationship by which eternal life is obtained. There is an eternal "if" in every consideration of eternal security.

But if we walk in the light...the blood of Jesus Christ his son cleanseth us from all sin (1 John 1:7). ...If that which ye have heard from the beginning shall remain in you, ye also shall continue in the Son, and in the Father (I John 2:24). ...if any man draw back, my soul shall have no pleasure in him (Hebrews 10:38). If a man abide not in me, he is cast forth as a branch, and is withered; and men gather them, and cast them into the fire... (John 15:6). ...if a man keep my saying, he shall never see death (John 8:51). ...if thou continue in his goodness: otherwise thou also shalt be cut off (Romans 11:22). ...if ye do these things, ye shall never fall (2 Peter 1:10). For we are made partakers of Christ, if we hold the beginning of our confidence stedfast unto the end (Hebrews 3:14). ...if we deny him, he also will deny us (2 Timothy 2:12). For if we sin wilfully after that we have received the knowledge of the truth, there remaineth no more sacrifice for sins (Hebrews 10:26). ...If any man love the world, the love of the Father is not in him (1 John 2:15). Ye are my friends, if ye do whatsoever I command you (John 15:14). For if ye live after the flesh, ye shall die (Romans 8:13).

All of these Scriptures are conditional, If we, as men, take our responsibility in the plan of salvation, God's sovereignty certainly holds no flaws.

All of the Scriptures fit in their proper place when we look at them in a balanced perspective. We do not have to throw any of them out to make our doctrine fit. There are Scriptures directed to those who are in danger of falling away, others which are directed to those who have no hope and have sinned unto death; some are for those who have overcome and therefore cannot fall from grace, and still others are directed to those who are striving to reach that place. Looking at the Scriptures in this light, we can see they do not contradict one another.

We should be encouraged not to turn back, as we are only

saved through faith in Jesus Christ as Saviour. **...There is none other name under heaven given among men, whereby we must be saved (Acts 4:12).** However, we show our faith by our works. It is a manifestation of our love for Him. Keeping God's commandments and doing right are merely the result of His Holy Spirit dwelling in the heart. These are the fruits of the Holy Spirit. We do these things not to be saved, but because we are saved.

As long as we love the Lord with all of our heart, we are going to be obedient to Him and cling to Him. He will not let go of us unless we cast Him away through our continued sin and indifference. We cannot lose our salvation, but we can forfeit it. Satan (Lucifer) lost his estate through willful sin. Adam and Eve lost their estate also because they sinned and fell from God's original plan. Jesus made a way for mankind to be restored simply because man did not have the light. Lucifer had full knowledge when he sinned; Adam and Eve were not walking in full knowledge when they sinned, so God made a way for them to be restored to their original place in God through Jesus Christ.

Let us not forget what we have in Christ but press on so that we do not end up shipwrecked.

Holding faith, and a good conscience; which some having put away concerning faith have made shipwreck (1 Timothy 1:19). And Jesus said unto him, No man, having put his hand to the plough, and looking back, is fit for the kingdom of God (Luke 9:62).

Transformation Through Obedience

We can complete our salvation by seeking God to cleanse us and perfect us to become like Jesus. This is accomplished by learning and obeying the Word of God. **For in many things we offend all. If any man offend not in word, the same is a perfect man, and able also to bridle the whole body (James 3:2).** Becoming like Jesus ultimately leads us into sonship with God. We

21

are not full grown when we first come into the knowledge of the Lord; however, we have the power within to accomplish this if we are willing. **But as many as received him, to them gave he power to become the sons of God, even to them that believe on his name: Which were born, not of blood, nor of the will of the flesh, nor of the will of man, but of God (John 1:12-13).**

If we are to become an overcomer and a son of God, we must do the will of God. The will of God is recorded in His Word, so we can see that as we learn and obey the Word of God this transformation will take place within us. What causes confusion for some of us is that we have been taught we are all equal in the Lord and that no one is any greater than another. Because of this we have failed to strive for the high calling in Christ. True, we are all equally loved by God and He offers all of His gifts and graces to all of mankind. However, these are conditional and only those who are willing to appropriate those things offered will mature in God.

During the millennial reign, Christians will serve God at various levels. These will be determined by their growth in Christ prior to that time. Since we are rapidly approaching the Kingdom age, the Lord is speaking to all who desire to rule and reign with Him. He is saying we must prepare if we want to be an overcomer, as only those who have entered into that place of maturity will inherit throneship. Other Christians will have a part in the kingdom, but only the overcomers will rule and reign with Him. **And he that overcometh, and keepeth my works unto the end, to him will I give power over the nations: And he shall rule them with a rod of iron; as the vessels of a potter shall they be broken to shivers: even as I received of my Father. And I will give him the morning star. He that hath an ear, let him hear what the Spirit saith unto the churches (Revelation 2:26-29).**

If we have not learned to overcome in our own vessels, how can we possibly rule other vessels? We must ask the Lord to cleanse us and remake us in His image if we desire to be an overcomer.

Being an overcomer does not make us more loved; however, we would have more authority than others because the Lord gives His authority only to those who know how to use it properly. Our position in the kingdom will be determined by how much of Jesus Christ and His Word is formed in us. **Whosoever therefore shall break one of these least commandments, and shall teach men so, he shall be called the least in the kingdom of heaven: but whosoever shall do and teach them, the same shall be called great in the kingdom of heaven (Matthew 5:19).**

Even now some Christians have advantages over others because they have appropriated more of the Word of God. Simply knowing the Word of God does not give us an advantage, for we must act upon and obey the Word if we are to walk in maturity. The reason there are so few victorious Christians is that this important teaching has been sorely neglected. Salvation does not depend upon becoming an overcomer, as many shall be in heaven who have not attained to the fullness of Christ. However, when one does become an overcomer, he will enter into the rest of God and know with assurance that he cannot fall away. **For as many as are led by the Spirit of God, they are the sons of God. For ye have not received the spirit of bondage again to fear; but ye have received the Spirit of adoption, whereby we cry, Abba, Father. The Spirit itself beareth witness with our spirit, that we are the children of God: And if children, then heirs; heirs of God, and joint-heirs with Christ; if so be that we suffer with him, that we may be also glorified together (Romans 8:14-17).**

As a son of God, we become a joint heir of all that He is and has.

We should not allow those out of balance "Manifested Sons of God" teachings to hinder us from pressing on to the high calling in Christ. **I press toward the mark for the prize of the high calling of God in Christ Jesus. Let us therefore, as many as be perfect, be thus minded: and if in anything ye be otherwise minded, God shall reveal even this unto you (Philippians 3:14-15).**

23

Those who have truly entered into a sonship position in Christ will not have to declare that position as it will be evident. If Christ is truly manifested in any person's life, the body of Christ will recognize it. Simply declaring it does not make it so.

Men of all ages have brought forth strange doctrines that do not agree with the Word of God. We must test them and take that which is truth, yet discard that which is error. Many of the wild ideas advanced by end-times groups are really void of the truth of God. However, we should not throw out all new revelation without testing it because God is bringing forth and restoring many beautiful truths at this hour.

One of those truths is the perfecting of the body of Christ. **And he gave some, apostles; and some, prophets; and some, evangelists; and some, pastors and teachers; For the perfecting of the saints, for the work of the ministry, for the edifying of the body of Christ: Till we all come in the unity of the faith, and of the knowledge of the Son of God, unto a perfect man, unto the measure of the stature of the fulness of Christ: That we henceforth be no more children, tossed to and fro, and carried about with every wind of doctrine, by the sleight of men, and cunning craftiness, whereby they lie in wait to deceive; But speaking the truth in love, may grow up into him in all things, which is the head, even Christ (Ephesians 4:11-15).**

We must realize that God wants us to walk in His fullness if we are to be overcomers.

That Christ may dwell in your hearts by faith; that ye, being rooted and grounded in love, May be able to comprehend with all saints what is the breadth, and length, and depth, and height; And to know the love of Christ, which passeth knowledge, that ye might be filled with all the fulness of God. Now unto him that is able to do exceeding abundantly above all that we ask or think, according to the power that worketh in us, Unto him be glory in the church by Christ Jesus throughout all ages, world without end. Amen (Ephesians 3:17-21).

The Inheritance of God

Walking in the fullness of God and inheriting all things does not mean that we shall inherit great material wealth. A true overcomer would not go about "claiming" material wealth. An overcomer will have arrived at the same place Paul attained when he said,

...for I have learned, in whatsoever state I am, therewith to be content. I know both how to be abased, and I know how to abound: every where and in all things I am instructed both to be full and to be hungry, both to abound and to suffer need. I can do all things through Christ which strengtheneth me (Philippians 4:11-13).

Stressing material possessions to the degree that our attention is no longer on God is just as out of balance as stressing sacrifice to the point of asceticism. One produces lust and materialism, while the other breeds fear and poverty. Materialism and self-imposed martyrdom are both evils.

Remove far from me vanity and lies: give me neither poverty nor riches; feed me with food convenient for me: Lest I be full, and deny thee, and say, Who is the Lord? or lest I be poor, and steal, and take the name of my God in vain (Proverbs 30:8-9).

Our lifestyles should not reflect the most expensive and extravagant clothes, diamonds, homes, cars, etc. This is not referring to well-dressed men and women and nice homes, but the extremes which reveal anything but the nature of Christ. Of course, neither is the other extreme of poverty the nature of Christ. We should live temperate, moderate lives, overcoming poverty and avoiding extreme wealth.

Jesus always went about giving to the poor. He never stored up His wealth even though He apparently handled a lot of money, thus the need for a treasurer, Judas. He gave away the things He could have used on Himself, yet He never lacked as He went about ministering. He should be our example today. Affection and lust for the things of this world do not portray the Spirit of Christ.

Paul had come to the place where he was not intimidated by his surroundings. If he was abased, he did not complain; if he was abounding, he did not flaunt his provisions but rather shared with others. The character of God remained evident in his life no matter what outward circumstances prevailed.

If it was necessary for him to endure suffering and poverty on the behalf of others, he gladly gave of himself. Paul had come to the place where men's words of praise did not cause him to be exalted with pride, nor did their criticisms disturb his composure. He had truly overcome the words of men as well as the money of men. His only desire was to please God.

In Christ, those who are now suffering under poverty need to count themselves rich, and those who are rich should count themselves poor. As God's people minister to one another the Lord desires that none lack in His kingdom. We are to help one another and give of our abundance to those who have needs.

But by an equality, that now at this time your abundance may be a supply for their want, that their abundance also may be a supply for your want: that there may be equality: As it is written, He that had gathered much had nothing over; and he that had gathered little had no lack (2 Corinthians 8:14-15).

The Lord desires for us to live full joyous lives and enjoy the good things He has created.

Some people refuse many things thinking that God would have them deny themselves any thing that would bring pleasure, believing all such things to be of the devil. Others make no sacrifices at all for the kingdom as they claim only the privileges and possessions of God. Both approaches are out of balance. We should be willing to sacrifice when the occassion calls for it, and we should also enjoy the blessings of God when they are bestowed upon us. To receive from other members of the body of Christ is sometimes difficult, but we must learn to receive as well as to give.

God's Attitude Toward Money

When we understand God's attitude toward wealth, we can then better understand the principles in His Word regarding money. There are approximately 700 direct references to money in the Bible and many more indirect references. Nearly two thirds of all the parables of Christ deal with the use of money. As we study His Word, we find as we progress that God relates our view of wealth with our commitment to Him. Let us look at His Word and see what God has to say about giving, for many Christians are unbalanced in this area.

Most Christians have been taught to give at least a tithe (10%) unto the Lord's work. This Scriptural pattern comes from the Old Testament law that commanded God's people to tithe of all that they received. **And all the tithe of the land, whether of the seed of they land, or of the fruit of the tree, is the Lord's: it is holy unto the Lord (Leviticus 27:30).** The people who obeyed the Lord and kept this commandment were blessed, but those who disobeyed suffered the curse. We can reap this same blessing to-day by giving a tenth unto the Lord's work and the support of His workers. **And, behold, I have given the children of Levi all the tenth in Israel for an inheritance, for their service which they serve, even the service of the tabernacle of the congregation (Numbers 18:21).**

Another tithe in the Old Testament was given unto the poor. Along with these two was a third that was to be used by the people so that they could go to the temple or tabernacle of the Lord and worship and praise Him **(Deuteronomy 14:22-29)**. Actually all faithful Jews were giving 30% in tithes, even before they began to give an offering that would be above the tithes. They experienced the blessings of God because of their faithfulness, but those who robbed God experienced the curse. **Will a man rob God? Yet ye have robbed me. But ye say, Wherein have we robbed thee? In tithes and offerings. Ye are cursed with a curse: for ye** have robbed me, even this whole nation. Bring ye all the tithes into the storehouse, that there may be meat in mine house, and prove me now herewith, saith the Lord of hosts, if I will not open you the windows of heaven, and pour you out a blessing, that there shall not be room enough to receive it. And I will rebuke the devourer for your sakes, and he shall not destroy the fruits of your ground; neither shall your vine cast her fruit before the time in the field, saith the Lord of hosts. And all nations shall call you blessed: for ye shall be a delightsome land, saith the Lord of hosts (Malachi 3:8-12).

Some believe that tithing is strictly Old Testament and we are not obligated to keep these laws today. Yet, if we look at Jesus' words He tells us in **Matthew 5:17, Think not that I am come to destroy the law, or the prophets: I am not come to destroy, but to fulfill.** In fact, in the New Testament we are held to even greater obligations because we now have the law written upon our hearts and have been given the power of the Holy Spirit to keep these higher laws. **But woe unto you, Pharisees! for ye tithe mint and rue and all manner of herbs, and pass over judgment and the love of God: these ought ye to have done, and not to leave the other undone (Luke 11:42).**

Tithing is really an elementary principle in the Word of God. Christians, filled with the Spirit of God, should be giving 100% to God. We are not to just allocate 10% to God, but we are to give everything we have to God without reservations. Then, as we bring these offerings to God, He will speak to us what He desires, not only in the area of money, but in all areas of our lives. As we give Him 100%, He will then instruct us in the ways we are to spend all of our money.

He will allocate funds for our households and businesses, as He knows these are necessary to our welfare. If we have difficulty in hearing the Lord in regard to the amount of our offering to God's work, the tithe would be the place to start until we can grow to understand His will in this area. He has always blessed those people who have given 10 percent to His work. When we give to God first, we find God makes the other 90 percent to more than cover our needs if we will but trust Him. He will also tell us where to give our offerings if we seek Him diligently. Giving the tithe (10%) shows our faith toward God in that the other 90% belongs to Him.

In the Old Testament, they brought their tithes and offerings to the storehouse and then were fed from there. Today we can bring our offerings to those places where we are being fed the Word of God. Other tithes were taken to the temple. Today we are the temple of the Holy Spirit and as we take our offerings before the Lord in the temple of our hearts, He will tell us where we are to give.

Giving Unto God

Some people believe they are not responsible after they give an offering as to whether it is being misused by the church or minister. This is not true, as we should seek God carefully in the area of wise giving or Satan can influence us to give to the wrong things and thus rob God's kingdom of money. There are several ways Satan does this. One is to get us to give to ministries who are not supporting true works of God. Another is to get people to give to fleshly ministries who are building their own kingdom instead of the kingdom of God.

And a certain ruler asked him, saying, Good Master, what shall I do to inherit eternal life? And Jesus said unto him, Why callest thou me good? none is good, save one, that is, God. Thou knowest the commandments, Do not commit adultery, Do not kill, Do not steal, Do not bear false witness, Honour thy father and thy mother. And he said, All these have I kept from my youth up. Now when Jesus heard these things, he said unto him, yet lackest thou one thing: sell all that thou hast, and distribute unto the poor, and thou shalt have treasure in heaven: and come, follow me. And when he heard

this, he was very sorrowful: for he was very rich. And when Jesus saw that he was very sorrowful, he said, How hardly shall they that have riches enter into the kingdom of God! For it is easier for a camel to go through a needle's eye, than for a rich man to enter into the kingdom of God" (Luke 18:18-25).

This man's love for his riches kept him not only from entering into the kingdom of God, but also from being one of His disciples.

The Lord went to the heart of this man's problem--not his money and riches, but his greater love for them than for Jesus. For the love of money is the root of all evil: which while some coveted after, they have erred from the faith, and pierced themselves through with many sorrows (1 Timothy 6:10). Would we be able to make this commitment today? If not, then we are in danger of missing God's blessings for our lives. We can "err from the faith" unless we are willing to follow God all the way.

Leaving All for Christ

Abraham is a perfect example of a man of faith who followed God wherever He called. **Hebrews 11:8-10** says,

By faith Abraham, when he was called to go out into a place which he should after receive for an inheritance, obeyed; and he went out, not knowing whither he went. By faith he sojourned in the land of promise, as in a strange country, dwelling in tabernacles with Isaac and Jacob, the heirs with him of the same promise: For he looked for a city which hath foundations, whose builder and maker is God. Here Abraham is recorded along with the other great faith patriarchs in this faith chapter of the New Testament.

Abraham passed one of the greatest tests of faith when he offered up Isaac unto the Lord. He was able to pass this test because previously he had been obedient to answer God's call. God spoke to him to leave all and go to a land he didn't know since this was part of God's plan for his life. Abraham was a wealthy man in his day, so he left a huge estate and many comforts by obeying God in this command. For many years he would live as a nomad in tents with no permanent dwelling place.

The reason he was able to do this was that Abraham had something that all disciples of Christ must have if they are to live the crucified life. He had heavenly vision. His eyes were not on the inheritance of the land he was journeying through, but his eyes were on God. He was looking for a city built by God.

Today, if we are to win our faith victories we must keep our eyes on Jesus.

One danger that can cause us not to receive our promise is keeping our eyes on our vision instead of on Jesus. We can then be deceived by the enemy because we may receive a true vision from God, but the timing may be many years in the future for this vision to come to pass; and when we do not see it materialize right away, we can become discouraged and lose faith.

If our eyes are on Jesus, He will sustain us and keep us busy until the day we just walk into the vision He gave us. We must have heavenly vision as Abraham did. The Word of God declares in **Proverbs 29:18, Where there is no vision, the people perish.**

Today the Lord is calling many to do the same thing Abraham did -- to leave all and follow him. This call does not generally go forth until other acts of obedience have been kept and demonstrated by the believer.

Some people act prematurely on a "call" from God and step out too soon instead of waiting for God to direct and make a way. The call is valid, but many times we need to wait on God's timing and training before we walk prematurely in a place God is not yet wanting us to go.

When Abraham's call came, he already had many years of experience in following God before he took this step of faith.

The Hundredfold Return

Should we receive the call today to leave all and follow him, we will know the blessings of promise that will accompany that call. **Mark 10:28-31** says,

Then Peter began to say unto him (Jesus), Lo, we have left all, and have followed thee. And Jesus answered and said, Verily I say unto you, There is no man that hath left house, or brethren, or sisters, or father, or mother, or wife, or children, or lands, for my sake, and the gospel's, But he shall receive an hundredfold now in this time, houses, and brethren, and sisters, and mothers, and children, and lands, with persecutions; and in the world to come eternal life. But many that are first shall be last; and the last first.

To understand the true significance of this passage, we must note several things. It is directed to those who leave all (this includes the willingness to leave their loved ones spiritually or even actually leaving them at times, as God directs, and receiving many loved ones in return). This Scripture is primarily directed to those who want to go all the way with Jesus and live the crucified life and be His disciples. The hundredfold blessing is promised here in the form of houses (of people) and lands (of people).

We must not take this out of context and claim a hundredfold blessing to mean physical lands and houses since the rest of the verse refers to brethren, sisters, mothers and children. Using this verse to claim a 100% material return on all of our giving is contrary to the rest of God's Word.

One rule we should follow when considering giving is to never give under emotional persuasion. Many fleshly ministries use not only emotional appeals, but also many other gimmicks to influence people to give to their ministries. Many people have given under this kind of pressure and later have found that it was not the Lord. Others have made pledges under the same influence and then have found they were unable to keep them. Any minister that would threaten people with the wrath of God should they fail to keep their pledge is definitely not under the Holy Spirit's leadership.

Pledges are very similar to vows or oaths unto God, and we are told not to swear in the New Testament. **But above all things, my brethren, swear not, neither by heaven, neither by the earth, neither by any other oath: but let your yea be yea; and your nay, nay; lest ye fall into condemnation (James 5:12).** We can desire to do certain things and tell the Lord that we want to be able to do them, but we should not promise God we will do them because Satan will condemn us if we should fail. This is not only true in the area of giving money, but also in other areas of our lives. We can make commitments to God, but not vows.

We should ask God who is worthy to receive the things He would have us bring as an offering unto Him. True ministers of God will receive offerings as unto the Lord and will not spend half their time begging, pleading, threatening or coercing people to give. Those ministers who are walking in faith know that God is their source and they do not look to people. God touches people's hearts to give when a minister is trusting God for his needs.

When we give unto the Lord, it should be with a cheerful attitude. If we give generously, the Lord blesses us in the same way. However, God's blessings don't come back only monetarily, but in the form of our needs when we are trusting Him.

But this I say, He which soweth sparingly shall reap also sparingly; and he which soweth bountifully shall reap also bountifully. Every man according as he purposeth in his heart, so let him give; not grudgingly, or of necessity: for God loveth a cheerful giver. And God is able to make all grace abound toward you; that ye, always having all sufficiency in all things, may abound to every good work: (As it is written, He hath dispersed abroad; he hath given to the poor: his righteousness remaineth for ever. Now he that ministereth seed to the sower both minister bread for your food, and multiply your seed sown, and increase the fruits of your righteousness;)

Being enriched in every thing to all bountifulness, which causeth through us thanksgiving to God. For the administration of this service not only supplieth the want of the saints, but is abundant also by many thanksgivings unto God (2 Corinthians 9:6-12).

Sowing and reaping is a very important principle in the Word of God. We must sow (plant) money into God's works if we expect to receive a harvest.

The Lord gives us money for two purposes. We must have money for a living and to eat plus money for giving. **For as the rain cometh down, and the snow from heaven, and returneth not thither, but watereth the earth, and maketh it bring forth and bud, that it may give seed to the sower, and bread to the eater (Isaiah 55:10).**

God expects us to keep money for bread as well as seed for sowing. Those Christians who give it all away and then expect God to take care of them are violating this principle of keeping bread to eat. (Farmers kept grain to grind into flour for bread making as well as some grain for seed to plant the next crop.) Some people give all their seed away and have nothing to eat, while others wrongly eat all their seed and have nothing to plant for the next harvest. We should have seed for both purposes.

After we plant a crop we expect a harvest; even so we should expect God to meet our financial needs when we have been obedient and have given of our tithes and offerings. **Give, and it shall be given unto you; good measure, pressed down, and shaken together, and running over, shall men give into your bosom. For with the same measure that ye mete withal it shall be measured to you again (Luke 6:38).**

Our giving should also be to help our brothers and sisters whenever the Lord so directs. We must learn how to give by the Spirit's direction and not allow our emotions or sympathy to rule us. Until we have had these soulish areas renewed, we can still be influenced by Satan through them. God is not always sympathetic with seemingly good causes. We should not give mechanically to things because it has been our pattern in times past, but we should remain open to the Lord's direction for our giving as with all guidance. Sometimes the Lord may speak that we are not to give to a certain person or ministry. We need to be just as sensitive to the Lord's restraining voice as to His condoning voice. He may want us to give elsewhere.

If we are truly walking in the Spirit, we will always have the desire to give because it is the nature of God to give. Greed and stinginess are from Satan. If we are truly committed to God, giving will not be a burden, but rather a joy. God is calling us to be committed to the point where if He told us to leave all and follow Him, we would not hesitate. We find a rich man in the Bible that could not make this commitment, and he ultimately missed God's blessings for his life.

The Lord is saying here that when we are serving him totally, we must deny even our own families in many ways. However, we will receive many new members in our family in the form of precious brothers and sisters in the Lord. We will be blessed by many people allowing us to share their homes and their land.

Many times as we travel for the Lord we are blessed in this way. So many people have said these words as we have entered their homes, "Our house belongs to the Lord, so please make it your home as long as you need a place to stay." Our natural family may be small, but because we serve Jesus, He has increased our family to include a hundredfold blessing in giving us many mothers, sisters, children and brethren.

The Lord does say with the blessings will come persecutions. Most of the time these persecutions come in the form of our being misunderstood by the message we bring. So many people do not know the power and gifts of the Holy Spirit and will talk against some of the most beautiful promises in the Word of God. We must pray for them, as we too once were walking in darkness and could not see. We can see that the Lord says many who are last shall be first and many who are first shall be last. This is a beautiful picture of those who have a servant's heart and don't mind being last, who will be promoted by the Lord to a higher position.

Looking at other Scriptures in reference to the word "hundredfold," we find in **Matthew 13:23, But he that received seed into the good ground is he that heareth the word, and understandeth it; which also beareth fruit, and bringeth forth, some an hundredfold, some sixty, some thirty.** This parable tells us that the seed is the Word of God and the good ground is an honest and good heart which will produce fruit. The fruit is the fruit of the Spirit in **Galatians 5:22, But the fruit of the Spirit is love, joy, peace, longsuffering, gentleness, goodness, faith, Meekness, temperance: against such there is no law.**

The Lord wants His righteousness produced in us in hundredfold amounts. This cannot be referring to money since money cannot be sown in our hearts. The Lord is cleansing us by His Word so that we can produce the fruit of the Spirit. **John 15:1-5** says,

I am the true vine, and my Father is the husbandman. Every branch in me that beareth not fruit he taketh away: and every branch that beareth fruit, he purgeth it, that it may bring forth more fruit. Now ye are clean through the word which I have spoken unto you. Abide in me, and I in you. As the branch cannot bear fruit of itself, except it abide in the vine; no more can ye, except ye abide in me. I am the vine, ye are the branches: He that abideth in me, and I in him, the same bringeth forth much fruit: for without me ye can do nothing. If we will notice closely here, this Scripture speaks of bearing fruit, more fruit and much fruit (30-fold, 60-fold, 100-fold). He wants us to bring forth much fruit as overcomers.

Abraham was an overcomer and he overcame by his faith in the Lord. We, too, can be overcomers and have the faith of Abraham if we allow the Lord to produce the fruit of faith in us until it bears a hundredfold. The "hundredfold return" is actually the fulness of God given to us in the form of our need. It can be money if that is our need because hundredfold faith can produce the money we need for the kingdom's sake. However, the real emphasis of **Mark 10:28-31** is when a man gives his all to God, God gives His all to him.

In looking again at **2 Corinthians 9:10**, we find the same truth expressed, **Now he that ministereth seed to the sower both minister bread for your food, and multiply your seed sown, and increase the fruits of your righteousness...** As we learn to give in every area of our lives including money, we find that the Lord will provide our needed bread and multiply that which we have sown so that we see the fruits of righteousness increase in our lives. When we give, the Lord stresses character increases, and seldom monetary increases. A monetary increase is simply the added blessing of our increase in righteousness. Should we need a hundredfold increase in money for the kingdom's sake, God will supply, but in accordance with our soul's state of being. **Beloved, I wish above all things that thou mayest prosper and be in health, even as thy soul prospereth (3 John 2).**

We should guard our motives and give out of love for the Lord, never giving to get back from Him. The world's kind of giving is always based on what we hope to get in return. God's giving is selfless and seeks no return. Above all else, God is concerned with our attitude toward money and our giving. He does not want our abundance or our lack of money to affect our relationship with Him in an adverse way. We are to trust God for all of our needs.

As for me, I will behold thy face in righteousness: I shall be satisfied, when I awake, with thy likeness (Psalm 17:15). He that trusteth in his riches shall fall: but the righteous shall flourish as a branch (Proverbs 11:28). Riches profit not in the day of wrath: but righteousness delivereth from death (Proverbs 11:4). Lay not up for yourselves treasures upon the earth, where moth and rust doth corrupt, and where thieves break through and steal: But lay up for yourselves treasures in heaven, where neither moth nor rust doth corrupt, and where thieves do not break through nor steal: For where your trea-

sure is, there will your heart be also (Matthew 6:19-21). God wants our hearts centered on Him and not on the things of this world. When we can simply use the things of this world and not allow them to consume our time and our hearts, then the Lord does not mind giving us material blessings. It is only when those things hold a place in our hearts above Him that they become displeasing.

Financial Problems

If we are having problems in the area of our finances, we need to examine God's Word as to what He says about finances and then line up with that Word. Are we handling our money wisely? Some Christians are giving too much to God's work in an attempt to please Him, yet are not paying their bills. It would be wise for them just to give a tithe for awhile until the Lord showed them how to pay their debts. Giving 50% to God and not paying our bills is not in harmony with the Scriptures. **Owe no man any thing, but to love one another: for he that loveth another hath fulfilled the law (Romans 13:8).** The Lord wants us out of debt, then we will be able to give more to His Kingdom. Some Christians go to the other extreme and say when they are out of debt, then they will give. We must always put God first in our finances, then He will show us the way out of debt.

So many people in our day are having financial problems. Even wealthy men are concerned they will lose their riches because of inflation and the worth of the dollar in an unstable condition. People are contemplating bankruptcy and even suicide due to such heavy money pressures.

Is there an answer to all the money problems? Yes, the Bible has the answer to this problem as well as all others that face mankind. Briefly, we are going to write down a basic financial check list based on the Word of God. On this list we are going to look at some things that can block our financial blessings. As Christians, we are promised the blessings of God, not the curses of the devil. The promise of prosperity and blessing belongs to us, not the curse of poverty and fear. **Galatians 3:13-14** says, **Christ hath redeemed us from the curse of the law, being made a curse for us: for it is written, Cursed is every one that hangeth on a tree: That the blessing of Abraham might come on the Gentiles through Jesus Christ; that we might receive the promise of the Spirit through faith.**

Genesis 17:1-7 says, **And when Abram was ninety years old and nine, the Lord appeared to Abram, and said unto him, I am the Almighty God; walk before me, and be thou perfect. And I will make my covenant between me and thee, and will multiply thee exceedingly. And Abram fell on his face: and God talked with him, saying, As for me, behold, my covenant is with thee, and thou shalt be a father of many nations. Neither shall thy name any more be called Abram, but thy name shall be Abraham; for a father of many nations have I made thee. And I will make thee exceeding fruitful, and I will make nations of thee, and kings shall come out of thee. And I will establish my covenant between me and thee and thy seed after thee in their generations for an everlasting covenant, to be a God unto thee, and to thy seed after thee."**

From these Scriptures we see we receive the same blessings as Abraham because we are his seed. Therefore, our first step is to become a child of God, thus the seed of Abraham. Then, **Matthew 6:31-33** applies to us. **Therefore take no thought, saying, What shall we eat? or, What shall we drink? or, Wherewithal shall we be clothed? (For after all these things do the Gentiles seek:) for your heavenly Father knoweth that ye have need of all these things. But seek ye first the kingdom of God, and his righteousness; and all these things shall be added unto you.** We must give our lives totally to God and seek His righteousness, then all the things that the Gentiles (those in the world) are seeking will be added to us. What are those in the world seeking? Clothes, houses, food, etc. This is the very first step to financial blessings. However, there are many Christians who still have not gained the victory in finances due to other principles in God's Word that have been ignored. Let's ask ourselves some questions that will bring us financial freedom if we are agreeing with the Word of God in these matters.

A Financial Check List

1. Are we giving at least 10% which is the tithe? (If not, we are using God's money, and robbing Him.)

Malachi 3:10: Bring ye all the tithes into the storehouse, that there may be meat in mine house, and prove me now herewith, saith the Lord of hosts, if I will not open you the windows of heaven, and pour you out a blessing, that there shall not be room enough to receive it.

Matthew 23:23: Woe unto you, scribes and Pharisees, hypocrites! for ye pay tithe of mint and anise and cummin, and have omitted the weightier matters of the law, judgment, mercy, and faith: these ought ye to have done, and not to leave the other undone.

2. Are we giving our tithe to the church where we are being fed? (Offerings, above the tithe, may be given to the poor, good works, etc. Additional offerings may be given to the church and its five-fold ministries as listed in **Ephesians 4:11**; apostles, prophets, evangelists, pastors, and teachers.)

2 Corinthians 9:6-8: But this I say, He which soweth sparingly shall reap also sparingly; and he which soweth bountifully shall reap also bountifully. Every man according as he purposeth in his heart, so let him give; not grudgingly, or of necessity: for God loveth a cheerful giver. And God is able to make all grace abound toward you; that ye, always having all sufficiency in all things, may abound to every good work.

3. Are we giving to God first before paying other bills?

Proverbs 3:9-10: Honour the Lord with thy substance,

40

and with the firstfruits of all thine increase: So shall thy barns be filled with plenty, and thy presses shall burst out with new wine.

4. Are we indifferent to the needs of the poor?

Proverbs 28:27: He that giveth unto the poor shall not lack: but he that hideth his eyes shall have many a curse.

5. Are we going in debt for lustful things? Wants?

1 Timothy 6:6-10: But godliness with contentment is great gain. For we brought nothing into this world, and it is certain we can carry nothing out. And having food and raiment let us be therewith content.

6. Are we planning and budgeting our financial spending?

Luke 14:28-30: For which of you, intending to build a tower, sitteth not down first, and counteth the cost, whether he have sufficient to finish it? Lest haply, after he hath laid the foundation, and is not able to finish it, all that behold it begin to mock him, Saying, This man began to build, and was not able to finish.

7. Are we lazy or slothful on the job? (A day's work for a day's pay.)

Ecclesiastes 9:10: Whatsoever thy hand findeth to do, do it with thy might; for there is no work, nor device, nor knowledge, nor wisdom, in the grave, whither thou goest.

Proverbs 21:25: The desire of the slothful killeth him; for his hands refuse to labour.

8. Are we too generous in giving to others without paying our own bills?

Proverbs 3:27-28: Withhold not good from them to whom it is due, when it is in the power of thine hand to do it. Say not unto thy neighbour, Go, and come again, and to morrow I will give; when thou hast it by thee.

9. Are we being wasteful?

John 6:12: When they were filled, he said unto his disciples, Gather up the fragments that remain, that nothing be lost.

10. Do all our money and material things belong to God?

Luke 12:34: For where your treasure is, there will your heart be also.

11. Do we need the things we buy or are they luxuries?

Proverbs 21:17: He that loveth pleasure shall be a poor man: he that loveth wine and oil shall not be rich.

12. Are we selfish in our families, spending more on our own wants?

1 Corinthians 10:24: Let no man seek his own, but every man another's wealth.

13. Are we willing to sell or give away anything that God would tell us to?

Matthew 19:21-22: Jesus said unto him, If thou wilt be perfect, go and sell that thou hast, and give to the poor, and thou shalt have treasure in heaven: and come and follow me. But when the young man heard that saying, he went away sorrowful: for he had great possessions.

14. Have we paid our debts or made arrangements to do so when we are having difficulties?

Romans 13:8: Owe no man any thing, but to love one another: for he that loveth another hath fulfilled the law.

15. Have we been sowing money into the kingdom of God? We reap in proportion to what we have sown (a little or a lot).

Luke 6:38: Give, and it shall be given unto you; good measure, pressed down, and shaken together, and running over, shall men give into your bosom. For with the same measure that ye mete withal it shall be measured to you again.

16. Have we done our spiritual homework in fasting and prayer over our finances?

Isaiah 58:6,9: Is not this the fast that I have chosen? to loose the bands of wickedness, to undo the heavy burdens, and to let the oppressed go free, and that ye break every yoke? Then shalt thou call, and the Lord shall answer; thou shalt cry, and he shall say, Here I am. If thou take away from the

midst of thee the yoke, the putting forth of the finger, and speaking vanity.

17. Have we been hard on people who owe us money, demanding payment with no mercy?

Luke 6:34-36: And if ye lend to them of whom ye hope to receive, what thank have ye? for sinners also lend to sinners, to receive as much again. But love ye your enemies, and do good, and lend, hoping for nothing again; and your reward shall be great, and ye shall be the children of the Highest: for he is kind unto the unthankful and to the evil.

18. Are there other areas that could be blocking our finances such as any unforgiveness, disobedience, stubbornness, etc.?

Matthew 6:14-15: For if ye forgive men their trespasses, your heavenly Father will also forgive you: But if ye forgive not men their trespasses, neither will your Father forgive your trespasses.

19. Are we spending our money foolishly or are we being wise?

Proverbs 24:3-4: Through wisdom is an house builded; and by understanding it is established: And by knowledge shall the chambers be filled with all precious and pleasant riches.

20. Are we totally committed to God, no matter what is happening?

Psalm 34:1: I will bless the Lord at all times: His praise shall continually be in my mouth.

Philippians 4:4-7: Rejoice in the Lord alway: and again I say, Rejoice. Let your moderation be known unto all men. The Lord is at hand. Be careful for nothing; but in every thing by prayer and supplication with thanksgiving let your requests be made known unto God. And the peace of God, which passeth all understanding, shall keep your hearts and minds through Christ Jesus.

21. Do we lack faith in God as our total source?

Psalm 112:1-3: Praise ye the Lord. Blessed is the man

that feareth the Lord, that delighteth greatly in his commandments. His seed shall be mighty upon earth: the generation of
the upright shall be blessed. Wealth and riches shall be in his
house: and his righteousness endureth for ever.

22. Are we hoarding things through fear or greed?

**Luke 12:19-21: And I will say to my soul, Soul, thou hast
much goods laid up for many years; take thine ease, eat, drink,
and be merry. But God said unto him, Thou fool, this night
thy soul shall be required of thee: then whose shall those things
be, which thou hast provided? So is he that layeth up treasure for himself, and is not rich toward God.**

This is different from preparing for the future by saving and
storing at God's direction.

**Proverbs 30:24-25: There be four things which are little
upon the earth, but they are exceeding wise: The ants are a
people not strong, yet they prepare their meat in the summer.**

23. Are we seeking financial blessing instead of seeking God
and His will? (Wanting God's benefits, but not God's ways.)

**Matthew 15:8: This people draweth nigh unto me with
their mouth, and honoureth me with their lips; but their heart
is far from me.**

These are some of the major reasons we fail financially. We
may have been ignorant about some of these things until now.
The Bible says in **Hosea 4:6a: My people are destroyed for lack
of knowledge.** Many Christians are being destroyed financially
either because they are ignorant of God's knowledge or they refuse
to adhere to it. Don't be destroyed in this area of your life. Simply
repent of past failures and ask God to give you the grace and
strength to obey Him and do those things that His Word outlines.
You can be an overcomer and walk in victory. Remember to give
God some time. You have been doing it the world's way a number
of years, now give God an opportunity to prove Himself faithful.

Malachi 3:10 says to prove Him. **Bring ye all the tithes
into the storehouse, that there may be meat in mine house,
and prove me now herewith, saith the Lord of hosts, if I will**

not open you the windows of heaven, and pour you out a blessing, that there shall not be room enough to receive it.

Galatians 6:9 promises we shall reap what we sow. Just as a farmer plants a crop and then there is a growing season before the harvest, so it is with planting God's Word in our hearts. **And let us not be weary in well doing: for in due season we shall reap, if we faint not.** Don't faint! We are overcomers in Christ.

Remember, we are stewards of all that we own and we must give an account to God for it. **Romans 14:12** says, **So then every one of us shall give account of himself to God.**

If we want to be pleasing to the Lord with our money, we must begin today to be faithful in the small amounts; only then will we be faithful in the larger amounts God will entrust us with as we obey Him. How wonderful it will be to then hear the Lord's commendation recorded in **Matthew 25:21: His lord said unto him, Well done, thou good and faithful servant: thou hast been faithful over a few things, I will make thee ruler over many things: enter thou into the joy of thy Lord.**

Some are heaping treasures together in these last days while ignoring God and they will find such treasures are worthless.

Go to now, ye rich men, weep and howl for your miseries that shall come upon you. Your riches are corrupted, and your garments are motheaten. Your gold and silver is cankered; and the rust of them shall be a witness against you, and shall eat your flesh as it were fire. Ye have heaped treasure together for the last days (James 5:1-3).

Money cannot save us from the tribulation of these last days; only our trust and faith in God will see us through.

Acquiring Understanding

Trust in the Lord with all thine heart; and lean not unto thine own understanding. In all thy ways acknowledge him, and he shall direct thy paths (Proverbs 3:5-6). This Scripture does not mean we are not to have understanding of the things that are taking place in our lives, but rather that we are not to lean to human reasoning. God wants to enlighten our understanding as He has even promised to reveal the secret things of God to those who are His servants. **Surely the Lord God will do nothing, but he revealeth his secret unto his servants the prophets (Amos 3:7)**. The Lord wants those who are heeding His voice to have understanding. **Evil men understand not judgment: but they that seek the Lord understand all things (Proverbs 28:5).**

When circumstances occur in our lives that we do not understand, we need to ask the Lord to show us what is wrong. Many attribute all adversities to the devil trying to hinder them without doing any introspection to see what gave the devil the open door. Others go to the opposite extreme and do so much self-introspection that they get their eyes off Jesus. Both extremes are not of the Lord.

We should definitely examine ourselves to see where we have fallen short when we have been attacked by the enemy, but we must not fall into the trap of condemnation and self-analyis. We must leave it to God to show us our failures when we are ready to see them.

The Lord wants to bring us to the place where we are always one step ahead of the devil and therefore not surprised by his attacks. The Lord wants us to be prepared for Satan and overcome him.

Jesus was never faced with a surprise attack from the devil. He knew not only what was in men's hearts, but also knew the ones who would deny and betray Him. Paul also was aware of the things that awaited him in Jerusalem, but he was determined to go anyway. If we are caught off guard by Satan's attacks, we have not yet grown to the place of being an overcomer in Christ. Jesus had such a close relationship with the Father that He always knew of the devil's plans. We too can come to that place. **Thine hand shall find out all thine enemies: thy right hand shall find out those that hate thee (Psalm 21:8).**

If we are to grow in Christ, we should not just say we do not understand when faced with adverse circumstances, but we should seek the Lord for His understanding to see the lack on our part.

Medicine or God

Another area where Christians tend to get out of balance is when to take medicine and when to believe God for their healing. Actually there should not be any conflict, but some people wrongly equate taking medicine with lack of faith in God. Faith in God is not related to whether or not we take medicine. Faith is an attitude of our hearts. Are we trusting the doctor and the medicine to heal us, or are we trusting God to heal us? God does not mind us going to the doctor nor does He mind us taking medicine. In fact, when we have been attacked by the devil, we can use all the weapons we have available to overcome him. It is when we have our faith in man instead of in God that we are sinning. Doctors cannot heal. In fact, any doctor will admit this. They can only promote healing. The actual healing process itself is still a mystery to them. They have learned certain techniques that assist in this healing process, but true healing comes only from God.

When we are under an attack by the devil with sickness, the first thing we need to do is seek God as to what He would have us do. He may encourage us to stand and pray and He will bring the healing. On the other hand, He may impress us to go to the doctor. We should follow His leading and not feel condemned should we seek medical help along with His divine help. The Lord can use doctors and medicine to bring our healing about, or He can bring it about through divine healing. When doctors no longer can help, we can trust the Lord to bring the needed miracle.

A word of warning in the area of doctors. Seek God diligently in this area because many of the medical practices today have their roots in Eastern religion, the occult and New Age. One form of medicine has it's roots in Eastern religion with some having acupuncture and acupressure as a part of the treatment procedures. They also declare "the life is in the spine" whereas the Word of God says, **For the life of the flesh is in the blood (Leviticus 17: 11a).** A false "laying on of hands" could occur as they manipulate the spine.

There are many good men and women who are involved in wrong medical practices because they do not have Biblical light in these areas; however, as Christians we are forbidden to partake of things that do not line up with the Word of God.

The New Age philosophies have influenced all realms of the medical profession including naturopathic as well as holistic healing practices. Christians must use discernment. Many Christians are deceived into taking numerous herbal and strange remedies for their ills instead of looking to Jesus for healing and strength. Satan has left no area untouched by his influence as he has many inroads into medicine and medical practices.

Those in pagan cultures must renounce all curses and ties from the witch doctors as these doctors are totally used of the devil. At times they can bring temporary physical relief; however, one is brought under great spiritual bondage when he seeks the help of witch doctors.

As overcomers, we must look to God for our healing and realize there is no cure outside of Him. We can walk in divine health even as Jesus did.

The ideal is for us to walk in this divine health, but on our way to overcoming we may have some battles with sickness. Satan will try to continue to put his evil upon us until we have learned how to defeat him. We do not have to accept sickness since it is a part of the curse and in the Lord we receive the blessings. Healing and health are our covenant rights.

Eating Unto the Lord

With so much emphasis on proper eating and physical exercise here in America, it has caused many to examine their lifestyles. Many people have now become imbalanced by putting too much emphasis on the physical man while neglecting the spiritual man. The Lord desires this area also to be in balance as our physical condition, if it is not properly cared for, affects our spiritual condition.

The spiritual man should always be given top priority as its influence over the physical man is greater than the physical man's influence over it. **For bodily exercise profiteth little: but godliness is profitable unto all things, having promise of the life that now is, and of that which is to come (1 Timothy 4:8).** We need proper balance between neglecting our bodies and giving them too much attention.

One of the greatest sins in the United States is gluttony. Food has become the god of millions. Jesus has never been made "Lord of the Fork." The Word of God has much to say about man's eating habits. Many sicknesses that are plaguing mankind stem directly from unhealthy eating habits. How should Christians eat? Are all the so-called health foods the answer to our diet problem? The Word of God has the answer to our questions as to what is healthy for us to eat.

So many have been eating according to the tradition of men instead of seeing what God's Word says about this subject. If we do not eat by the Word of God, our eating habits will be dictated by the patterns of the country in which we were born. In Japan, mice are considered a delicacy; in South America, lizards are part of the menu and vultures are eaten in parts of Africa. These would be repulsive to the average American, and they are listed in the Word of God, along with some other scavengers commonly eaten here, as unclean abominations to God.

The eleventh chapter of Leviticus gives the complete list of unclean meats; we find that pork is also one mentioned. **And the swine, though he divide the hoof, and be clovenfooted, yet he cheweth not the cud; he is unclean to you. Of their flesh shall ye not eat... (Leviticus 11:7-8).** Other unclean meats commonly

49

eaten by Americans are shrimp, oysters, clams, crabs, lobsters, catfish, snails and froglegs. It is no wonder Americans are suffering with all kinds of sicknesses and diseases since they do not realize that their diets are contaminating their bodies.

Many Christians who are struggling to win their battle over illness do not realize that their diets could be one of the hindering factors preventing divine healing. There are those who have received divine healings, yet they find their old maladies return even after standing against the devil. They have not considered that a faulty diet could be the cause. The Bible says, **...the curse causeless shall not come (Proverbs 26:2).**

Many object to changing their diets as they feel they are free to eat anything, and they declare that the Old Testament laws are obsolete as we now live under grace. However, if we examine these objections closely in the light of God's Word, we see that they cannot stand. We need a basic understanding of the three types of laws given in the Old Testament before we discuss the dietary law. One is the moral law which is summed up in the Ten Commandments **(Exodus 20:1-17).** The second is the dietary law **(Leviticus 11 and Deuteronomy 14:3-21)** and other "physical laws" listed in these two books. The third is the ceremonial law **(Exodus 25-40 and the book of Leviticus).** All of these laws were given by God to Moses for His people Israel. They were for their good and their protection.

Obviously, we do not ignore the moral laws listed in the Ten Commandments today simply because they are in the Old Testament. They are just as valid for man's welfare now as they were then. This also applies to the physical and dietary laws. The ceremonial laws are the only ones we do not keep today since they were fulfilled in Christ Jesus. All of the spiritual ceremonies were types and shadows of the purpose and work of Christ bringing redemption to mankind **(Hebrews 9 and 10). In burnt offerings and sacrifices for sin thou hast had no pleasure. Then said I, Lo, I come (in the volume of the book it is written of me), to do thy will, O God. Above when he said, Sacrifice and offer-**

ing and burnt offerings and offering for sin thou wouldest not, neither hadst pleasure therein; which are offered by the law; Then said he, Lo, I come to do thy will, O God. He taketh away the first, that he may establish the second. By the which will we are sanctified through the offering of the body of Jesus Christ once for all (Hebrews 10:6-10). From this we see that spiritually we have been sanctified; if we have accepted Jesus as our Lord, we are spiritually cleansed by His blood.

The things we eat cannot defile us spiritually as they did the people in the Old Testament. If they ate any unclean thing, they could not enter the temple for worship. Today, we are not prevented from worshipping the Lord through the things we eat or don't eat. However, when we eat unclean things we do defile our physical bodies. Those who put people under legal bondage when they eat or don't eat certain things are violating the spiritual freedom we have in Christ. Eating wrongly, however, is a violation of certain physical laws that can consequently cause damage to our bodies.

Jesus never violated these laws as He kept the law perfectly and was the only man who ever did. That is why His life was the perfect sacrifice for man's sin. He declared in **Matthew 5:17, Think not that I am come to destroy the law, or the prophets: I am not come to destroy, but to fulfill.** For Christians, the Old Testament laws are not to be done away with; rather they have been amplified and in the New Testament we have been given higher laws. **This is the convenant that I will make with them after those days, saith the Lord, I will put my laws into their hearts, and in their minds will I write them (Hebrews 10:16).**

Keeping this in mind, let us examine some of the Scriptures in the New Testament that are commonly quoted in an attempt to allow us to eat anything.

Then came to Jesus scribes and Pharisees, which were of Jerusalem, saying, Why do thy disciples transgress the tradition of the elders? for they wash not their hands when they eat bread (Matthew 15:1-2). And he called the multitude, and

51

said unto them, Hear, and understand: Not that which goeth into the mouth defileth a man; but that which cometh out of the mouth, this defileth a man. Then came his disciples, and said unto him, Knowest thou that the Pharisees were offended, after they heard this saying? But he answered and said, Every plant, which my heavenly Father hath not planted, shall be rooted up. Let them alone: they be blind leaders of the blind. And if the blind lead the blind, both shall fall into the ditch. Then answered Peter and said unto him, Declare unto us this parable. And Jesus said, Are ye also yet without understanding? Do not ye yet understand, that whatsoever entereth in at the mouth goeth into the belly, and is cast out into the draught? But those things which proceed out of the mouth come forth from the heart; and they defile the man. For out of the heart proceed evil thoughts, murders, adulteries, fornications, thefts, false witness, blasphemies: These are the things which defile a man: but to eat with unwashen hands defileth not a man (Matthew 15:10-20).

Actually the subject of this Scripture is eating with unwashed hands. The Jews had a ceremonial law for cleansing things before eating. They were upset because Jesus did not observe this ceremony. (He did not because He was the fulfillment of that ceremony as He came to cleanse men from their sins.)

When Jesus spoke the words, "Not that which goeth into the mouth defileth a man; but that which cometh out of the mouth, this defileth a man," He was not referring to our being able to eat all foods, but was stressing that man is not spiritually defiled by eating with unwashed hands. Spiritual defilement comes from sin in men's hearts. He was stressing a spiritual truth and was disturbed with His disciples for not understanding what He was saying. He knew they were spiritually blind. This Scripture cannot be used to sanction the eating of all meats and foods for if these verses were taken literally today we would not wash our hands when we eat.

Other Scriptures that people quote to promote the idea that

unclean meats are now edible are those that describe Peter's vision of the unclean animals when the Lord spoke to him to take and eat of them. Let's look at those Scriptures to discern the Lord's true meaning.

On the morrow, as they went on their journey, and drew nigh unto the city, Peter went up upon the housetop to pray about the sixth hour: And he became very hungry, and would have eaten, but while they made ready, he fell into a trance, And saw heaven opened, and a certain vessel descending unto him, as it had been a great sheet knit at the four corners, and let down to the earth: Wherein were all manner of fourfooted beasts of the earth, and wild beasts, and creeping things, and fowls of the air. And there came a voice to him, Rise, Peter; kill, and eat. But Peter said, Not so, Lord; for I have never eaten anything that is common or unclean. And the voice spake unto him again the second time, What God hath cleansed, that call not thou common. This was done thrice: and the vessel was received up again into heaven. Now while Peter doubted in himself what this vision which he had seen should mean, behold, the men which were sent from Cornelius had made inquiry for Simon's house, and stood before the gate, And called, and asked whether Simon, which was surnamed Peter, were lodged there (Acts 10:9-18).

We notice from these verses that Peter was an obedient Jew who kept the dietary laws. That is why he could not understand the Lord telling him to eat something that was unclean according to the Word of God. He knew there must be a spiritual interpretation to the vision because he knew the Lord would not violate His Word.

The Lord revealed to Peter the meaning of his vision in **verse 28, And he said unto them, Ye know how that it is an unlawful thing for a man that is a Jew to keep company, or come unto one of another nation; but God hath shewed me that I should not call any man common or unclean...Of a truth I perceive that God is no respector of persons: But in every** nation he that feareth him, and worketh righteousness, is accepted with him (Acts 10:28, 34-35).

From these verses we see that the Lord was not saying that all animals were cleansed for eating, but that the Gentiles who were considered unclean were not to be despised or called common anymore.

The Lord had, until this time, only used the nation of Israel as His vessel for salvation. However, Jesus' death and resurrection ushered in a new dispensation so that other peoples and nations would now be included in God's plan if they received Him as their Saviour. **For there is no difference between the Jew and the Greek: for the same Lord over all is rich unto all that call upon him. For whosoever shall call upon the name of the Lord shall be saved (Romans 10:12-13).** Today, much emphasis is still put on the Jews as being God's chosen people. However, they are no longer the chosen ones; they are lost like everyone else unless they call upon the name of the Lord Jesus Christ. An out-of-balance stress upon watching the nation of Israel for our end-time timetable can create problems for Christians too. Spiritual Israel, born-again Christians, hold the key for the end times. Certain things must come to pass in the nation of Israel, but spiritual Israel is the one that will be restored and rebuilt in this last hour. She will come into her glory. Physical Israel is only the type, while spiritual Israel is the reality. Those expecting God to use the natural Jews in an end-time ministry will be disappointed since it is the spiritual Jew that will be used of God. Of course, any Jew who is born again will be used of God, but not any more than God's true chosen people who are those who have come to know Him as their Messiah.

For he is not a Jew, which is one outwardly; neither is that circumcision, which is outward in the flesh: But he is a Jew, which is one inwardly; and circumcision is that of the heart, in the spirit, and not in the letter; whose praise is not of men, but of God (Romans 2:28-29).

Peter knew his vision was not for cleansing meat, but rather was for the revelation of the Gentiles being cleansed as they received the message of salvation.

Another Scripture that we need to look at is found in **I Timothy 4:4-5, For every creature of God is good, and nothing to be refused, if it be received with thanksgiving: For it is sanctified by the word of God and prayer.** The word "sanctified" is usually overlooked in these verses. This word means "to cleanse." How do we cleanse those things we eat?--by the Word of God and prayer. If the Word of God says it is clean, we can eat it; if not, it is not considered clean. Then, we are to pray and thank God for our food before we eat as this also cleanses it for us. Especially today when so many of our foods are contaminated with preservatives, dyes and insecticides, we need to pray for the cleansing of our food. This Scripture is saying that all creatures that are sanctified (cleansed) by His Word and are of God are good to be eaten, but not all creatures inclusively, otherwise this verse would condone cannibalism.

Other portions of God's Word tell us as we keep His laws we shall benefit healthwise.

My son, forget not my law; but let thine heart keep my commandments: For length of days, and long life, and peace, shall they add to thee (Proverbs 3:1-2). Be not wise in thine own eyes: fear the Lord, and depart from evil. It shall be health to thy navel, and marrow to thy bones (Proverbs 3:7-8). My son, attend to my words; incline thine ear unto my sayings. Let them not depart from thine eyes; keep them in the midst of thine heart. For they are life unto those that find them, and health to all their flesh (Proverbs 4:20-22).

God has set up the whole universe on a foundation of laws that govern all of life on every plane, in every sphere and at every level. The entire universe is run by laws. All life operates according to laws. When man observes them, he benefits; when he abuses them, he suffers.

The dietary laws were not given to procure eternal life, but rather to preserve and bless man's earthly life. The highest law in the universe is the law of love. There are times we are to eat what is set before us since that would be the loving thing to do. When we dine with those who are not aware of God's dietary laws, we should not condemn them by refusing to eat, but simply ask God to cleanse it before we partake. We find this was the Lord's instructions to the seventy He sent out. **And into whatsoever city ye enter, and they receive you, eat such things as are set before you (Luke 10:8).** Jesus would not have commanded them to eat such things as were set before them unless they had been taught not to eat certain things. The Lord knew the Gentiles did not have the Word of God and therefore would be eating things that were unclean. Instead of preaching the lesser message of dietary laws, Jesus sent his disciples forth with the greater message of salvation. The people would eventually be exposed to all of God's Word, but the salvation message had first priority. The law of love would cover those things the disciples ate since they knew they were not under bondage to the letter of the law. Because the disciples' hearts were pure, the Lord would sanctify what they ate.

The Roman Christians had a problem with some of them eating meat that had been offered to idols. Paul instructed them in the way of love. He knew eating meat would not hurt them if their hearts were pure, but Paul stressed the higher law of love. If their eating would cause their brother to stumble, they should not do so.

For meat destroy not the work of God. All things indeed are pure; but it is evil for that man who eateth with offence. It is good neither to eat flesh, nor to drink wine, nor any thing whereby thy brother stumbleth, or is offended, or is made weak...And he that doubteth is damned if he eat, because he eateth not of faith: for whatsoever is not of faith is sin (Romans 14:20, 21, and 23).

Some just quote the portion of this Scripture that says, "All things indeed are pure" and use this to say we can eat anything. If we take the words "all things" to apply to everything, that would mean we could eat sticks, rocks and metal. Obviously these words mean all things approved of by God. His Word tells us what He approves and disapproves. Since these verses are referring to meats, we can go back to **Leviticus 11** to see which meats are approved.

The clean animals that chew the cud and have divided hooves, are the ox, sheep, goat, deer, cow, steer, buffalo, etc. These animals, because they chew the cud, completely process all vegetable matter they eat and cleanse it of any poisonous or deleterious matter before it becomes a part of their flesh. Therefore, when we eat these meats they are considered clean by God. The list of unclean meats, of which pork is the leader in consumption, fall into the general category of scavengers. The hog will eat any putrid thing he can find, as will catfish eating off the bottom of riverbeds. Shrimp, lobsters, crabs, clams and oysters are the ocean floor scavengers. All unclean animals feed on filth and this is what we ultimately take into our systems by eating them.

Coming from a medical background, I can personally testify to the numerous parasites that swine harbor, the worst being Trichinella spiralis. Trichinosis, the name for this disease, cripples and kills. Pains in joints can also be traced to this terrible disease caused by minute spiral worms. The possibility of this disease alone should cause people to leave pork out of their diets. More and more doctors are recommending the abstinence of pork as recent medical discoveries have traced even other diseases to this source. I personally have not eaten any pork for many years. I began this diet from a medical standpoint long before I knew it was the wisdom of the Lord.

This, of course, is only one portion of God's Word; but if we add it to the others, we will find we shall enjoy more of God's blessings. The blessing of health comes when we obey the Word of God. If we refuse, we suffer the consequences. If we continue to eat things that violate the Word of God and are an abomination to Him, how can we expect to walk in divine health? **They that sanctify themselves, and purify themselves in the gardens behind one tree in the midst, eating swine's flesh, and the**

abomination, and the mouse, shall be consumed together, saith the Lord (Isaiah 66:17).

What does God's Word say about other foods besides meats? A good guideline would be to eat "living foods." The natural, living foods are fresh vegetables, fruits, grains, meats and dairy products. The "dead foods" are those that are highly refined. They not only are expensive, but also in most instances do little to nourish. Many people are tired, run down and sick because a large part of their diets are made up of dead junk foods.

As we seek the Lord in regard to our diets, He will gladly lead us in the right path. We must not get out of balance in this area and let menus and cooking absorb an exorbitant amount of time since this would be just as bad as ignoring diet altogether and eating anything we want. However, we want to include at least an outline of some of God's approved foods to help people get started on the road to proper eating.

Some of God's Approved Food

Barley	Ruth 2:23
Bread	Luke 22:19
Butter	Isaiah 7:22
Corn	Ruth 2:14; I Samuel 17:17
Cheese	I Samuel 17:18
Dates	Genesis 3:2
Eggs	Job 6:6
Figs	Numbers 13:23; I Samuel 25:18
Fruits (all)	Genesis 1:29
Herbs (Leafy Plants) and Vegetables	Genesis 1:29
Honey	Deuteronomy 8:8
Meats: Beef	
Fish	
Mutton	
Poultry	
Venison	Deuteronomy 14; Leviticus 11

Milk	Isaiah 7:21-22
Nuts	Genesis 43:11
Olives and Olive Oil	Leviticus 2:4; Deuteronomy 8:8
Salt	Leviticus 2:13
Wheat	Psalm 81:16

Although this list is not complete, it does give the basic foods that the Lord calls clean for us to eat.

Leviticus 11 tells us all fish are clean if they have scales and fins. Most fish fall into this category except for the catfish, shark and dolphin families. Chicken, duck and turkey are considered clean, but all birds in the vulture family are unclean. God gave us His laws so that we would know how to eat wisely. Keeping these laws will not produce holiness nor gain us entry into heaven. However, we can benefit from them and be able to serve the Lord better if our physical bodies are in good shape. For further study on dietary laws, we recommend a good book entitled, God's Key to Health and Happiness by Elmer A. Josephson.

We must trust the creator to know what is best for us to eat, instead of eating according to our traditions. He not only made our bodies, but all the animals as well; and He certainly would not make the distinction between clean and unclean if it makes no difference what we eat. **1 Corinthians 10:31** sums it up beautifully, **Whether therefore ye eat, or drink, or whatsoever ye do, do all to the glory of God.** So in all our partaking of food or drink we must ask ourselves, "Is what I am doing pleasing to God? Will my diet nourish my body so that it will be efficient in His service? Will it make my mind keener, my muscles stronger, my judgment more sound, my influence for the Lord more potent?"

Some things that we drink are just as bad for our bodies as the food we eat. We all agree strong alcoholic beverages destroy the body as well as the mind. However, we need to look at all beverages that are addictive. Caffeine in any form is addictive, yet millions of Christians must have this stimulant to wake them in the morning, instead of relying on the strength of God that comes through prayer. Our children are addicted to the caffeine and white sugar found in soda pops. Satan has subtly paved the way for stronger addictions once our children are older.

Many Christians cry "bondage" when a change of diet is suggested. Could it be the flesh crying for its addiction? We must ask God to deliver us from every desire to eat or drink anything that would defile our temples. Not only should our spiritual temples be cleansed, but also our physical ones so that we might serve the Lord without any hindrances. Use of tobacco is another addictive defilement of our temples. If we really desire to become an overcomer, we will bring our bodies into subjection to the Holy Spirit as Paul did.

Know ye not that they which run in a race run all, but one receiveth the prize? So run, that ye may obtain. And every man that striveth for the mastery is temperate in all things. Now they do it to obtain a corruptible crown; but we an incorruptible. I therefore so run, not as uncertainly; so fight I, not as one that beateth the air: But I keep under my body, and bring it into subjection: lest that by any means, when I have preached to others, I myself should be a castaway (1 Corinthians 9:24-27).

End Time Revelations

Another area that causes conflict for Christians is an out-of-balance emphasis regarding end-time prophecies and revelations. Because we are living in the final days before the Lord Jesus Christ returns to this earth, it is understandable that this be of great interest and concern for us. However, the main problem for most Christians is the uncertain warning going forth. We hear on one hand that before the great tribulation begins the Lord is going to rapture the church away. Then we hear others proclaiming we are to prepare to go through the seven-year period of the great tribulation before the Lord finally comes. Finally, to make it even more confusing, others declare that the "catching away" of the saints is to occur at the middle of the tribulation after the Antichrist comes on the scene. What are we to believe? Who has the truth?

As Christians, we should not accept anything we hear as the truth until we have gone to the Holy Spirit (He is the Spirit of Truth) and examined it in the light of the Holy Scripture. One trap that many Christians fall into is to accept things simply because they have been taught that way and it has been the traditional teaching for many years. We must prove or test all things and this would especially apply to end-time revelations.

One of Satan's lies to Christians is that the book of Revelation is so far beyond their comprehension that they could not possibly understand it. None of us can understand the Word of God without the Holy Spirit's enlightenment. However, when He brings light, even the youngest Christian can see clearly.

We must not fall into the trap of only receiving our truths from others. Certainly God uses His ministers to bring light to us, but we are to receive light from Him as individual members of His body, too.

We can know and understand the mysteries of God if we will seek Him with our whole heart. **Then shall ye call upon me, and ye shall go and pray unto me, and I will hearken unto you. And ye shall seek me, and find me, when ye shall search for me with all your heart (Jeremiah 29:12-13).** The Lord will send someone with the truths we need to hear, and our hearts and spirits will witness to them as the Holy Spirit's light if we are having difficulty understanding. However, accepting things without testing them will open the door for error.

For instance, because the pre-tribulation rapture has been taught for many years, there are those who believe this to be truth although they have not personally sought the Lord and studied His Word to test this theory. Actually the term "rapture" is nowhere to be found in the Bible. Although there is Scripture that describes a "catching away," there are many more Scriptures that support the view that the church will be here for a time during the great tribulation. One of these is very clear as to Christ's coming. It is **Matthew 24:29-31.**

Immediately after the tribulation of those days shall the sun be darkened, and the moon shall not give her light, and the stars shall fall from heaven, and the powers of the heavens shall be shaken: And then shall appear the sign of the Son of man in heaven: and then shall all the tribes of the earth mourn, and they shall see the Son of man coming in the clouds of heaven with power and great glory. And he shall send his angels with a great sound of a trumpet, and they shall gather together his elect from the four winds, from one end of heaven to the other.

The real emphasis should not be focused on the time of Christ's second coming anyway. Our attention should be fixed upon our preparation for that coming. Are we ready to meet Him whenever he comes? If our attitude is simply concerned with the trials and tribulations of this life and the things that are coming upon the earth, then we are definitely not ready to meet Him. Many are using the "pre-trib rapture" as an escape mechanism. Fear is ruling their lives concerning the future and they see the rapture as a way out. They can leave their debts, troubles and sickness behind and go to be with the Lord.

The overcomer will not face the coming days with this attitude. He will not be fearful of anything as he knows the power of God will rest upon His people in the last days, and no matter what comes upon the world he will be safe under the protection of the Almighty. He knows that he can overcome anything through Christ. He knows the Word of God declares that the judgment is to come upon the wicked and nothing can harm those who are walking totally committed to the Lord. Therefore, he will not fear the great tribulation any more than he would fear any other tribulation. He will have learned to overcome the trials and tribulations of this life as a member of the kingdom of God. **Confirming the souls of the disciples, and exhorting them to continue in the faith, and that we must through much tribulation enter into the** kingdom of God (Acts 14:22). These things I have spoken unto you, that in me ye might have peace. In the world ye shall have tribulation: but be of good cheer; I have overcome the world (John 16:33).

The main thing for all Christians to do is to concentrate on the Holy Spirit's cleansing and preparing them for the day of His return.

The Scripture says He is coming back for a church that is holy and consecrated. If we are to qualify to be a part of His bride, we must be ready. **That he might present it to himself a glorious church, not having spot, or wrinkle, or any such thing; but that it should be holy and without blemish (Ephesians 5:27).** Satan uses the controversy over the time of Christ's return to separate the body of Christ. We should not be as concerned over the time as over our preparation. If we are ready, then we will not be troubled by the prospect of going through the great tribulation. The parable of the ten virgins **(Matthew 25)** is given to show us the emphasis should be upon preparation. All were virgins (the church), but not all were prepared. Only those with oil in their lamps could see the way to meet Him. The oil is symbolic of the Holy Spirit. Only those who are filled with the Holy Spirit will have the light needed to go and meet Him. Worldly Christians will find their lamps have gone out. This is a warning for us to be filled with the Holy Spirit and thus be ready for His coming.

The Lord has always protected His saints throughout Bible history if they were walking with Him and listening to Him. Noah is a classic example. The Bible calls him a perfect man.

...Noah was a just man and perfect in his generations, and Noah walked with God (Genesis 6:9). And God said unto Noah, The end of all flesh is come before me; for the earth is filled with violence through them; and, behold, I will destroy them with the earth. Make thee an ark of gopher wood... (Genesis 6:13-14).

Due to Noah's faith and obedience to God, he and all his

family were spared the judgment that came upon the earth. To-day, if we are walking with God in righteousness, we will have that same protection for us and our families.

We are warned by Jesus that judgment is coming upon the earth before He returns to gather His church. Yet if we are ready, we will have the safety of the ark even as Noah did.

But of that day and hour knoweth no man, no, not the angels of heaven, but my Father only. But as the days of Noah were, so shall also the coming of the Son of man be. For as in the days that were before the flood they were eating and drinking, marrying and giving in marriage, until the day that Noah entered into the ark, And knew not until the flood came, and took them all away; so shall also the coming of the Son of man be (Matthew 24:36-39).

Continuing in this Scripture in Matthew, we find the verses that those who believe in the pre-tribulation rapture use to support their position. **Then shall two be in the field; the one shall be taken, and the other left. Two women shall be grinding at the mill; the one shall be taken, and the other left (Matthew 24:40-41).** Many have assumed that it was the righteous ones taken and the others that were left, but in Noah's day it was the evil ones who were taken away and the righteous ones who were left protected in the ark.

In fact, in another of Jesus' parables we find Him teaching on this very thing.

Another parable put he forth unto them, saying, The kingdom of heaven is likened unto a man which sowed good seed in his field: But while men slept, his enemy came and and sowed tares among the wheat, and went his way. But when the blade was sprung up, and brought forth fruit, then appeared the tares also. So the servants of the householder came and said unto him, Sir, didst not thou sow good seed in thy field? from whence then hath it tares? He said unto them, An enemy hath done this. The servants said unto him, Wilt thou then that we go and gather them up? But he said, Nay;

lest while ye gather up the tares, ye root up also the wheat with them. Let both grow together until the harvest: and in the time of harvest I will say to the reapers, Gather ye together first the tares, and bind them in bundles to burn them: but gather the wheat into my barn (Matthew 13:24-30).

From this parable we see that first the evil ones (the tares) in the Master's field are gathered and destroyed, then the righteous ones (the wheat) are gathered.

Judgment is first to begin at the house of God, with the Lord removing those who look like wheat, but are false. Then He gathers the true wheat. **For the time is come that judgment must begin at the house of God: and if it first begin at us, what shall the end be of them that obey not the gospel of God? (1 Peter 4:17).** Those who do not submit themselves to the refining fire of the Lord for cleansing will be taken away. Perhaps we feel so far from perfection and that there is so much to be done in our lives that it looks impossible. Our God is the God of the impossible, and He delights in taking weak men and women and making them into His own image through the power of the Holy Ghost. We simply need to yield to Him so that He can do that work. Even if we are still immature in some areas of our lives, as we follow in the Lord's steps, He will accomplish the work that will eventually bring us into full stature.

God is working in different areas of our lives to mature us so we'll stand in full stature as full men in Christ Jesus. The purpose of the Holy Spirit coming into our lives is to conform us into the image of Jesus Christ. We're to look like Jesus, act like Jesus, talk like Jesus and do the works of Jesus. That's the intent of the Holy Spirit. Where are we? Do we look like Jesus? Are we talking like Jesus? Are we acting like Him? Well, we're pressing into that place, and some of us are stronger and more mature in certain areas of our lives than others. But in other areas we are still babies, and God is striving to mature us in our weak areas, dealing ever so gently and beautifully with us at our own pace.

He's so kind and patient. He doesn't try to change us all at once. He showed me a beautiful analogy that fits the parable of the tares and wheat. I was working in an area of the yard that had been newly planted with grass. The little baby grass was growing up, but the weeds were too, and they were way ahead of the grass. I thought, "That's just like our lives. We try to get the grass to grow, but the weeds are growing up twice as fast." I pulled up a few of the weeds from the patch of grass, and do you know what happened? I pulled up the baby grass. God then said, "Betty, sometimes I leave weeds in your life that are not ready to be uprooted until the grass gets a firm hold. And when the grass gets a firm hold, then I can go in and pull up the weeds. The weeds are not the problem. The problem is getting the grass to grow."

When our relationship is established with the Father in a strong, firm way, then it's no problem for Him to take a weed out because we are established in Him. But until we are established in Him, our lives remain a mixture of grass and weeds. Now, God doesn't want them there. He doesn't want weeds in our lives. But let us not be hard on one another in the Body of Christ while there are still weeds in one another's lives. Let's pray for one another and say, "God, help them, strengthen them and make them strong until the weeds can come out." Instead, much of the time we judge other's weaknesses from our own strengths. We shouldn't concentrate on the weeds, but on getting the grass to grow.

The Lord is coming back after a glorious church that will be walking in love and unity. We need to strengthen one another so we are ready for that day. The Lord wants us to be prepared and ready so that we are not caught unaware.

Watch therefore: for ye know not what hour your Lord doth come. But know this, that if the good man of the house had known in what watch the thief would come, he would have watched, and would not have suffered his house to be broken up. Therefore be ye also ready: for in such an hour as ye think not the Son of man cometh. Who then is a faithful and wise servant, whom his lord hath made ruler over his household, to give them meat in due season? Blessed is that

servant, whom his lord when he cometh shall find so doing (Matthew 24:42-46).

If we do not want to see our households divided by the devil and our loved ones ravaged, then we must be faithful and stand in faith for them. Even if they are walking in rebellion now, our faith can release them and bring them back to the Lord.

A good way to pray for those who are in a backslidden condition is to cut off Satan's supplies to them. If we pray the Lord's blessing over them and cut off Satan's supplies, then it will be easier for them to return to God. However, if Satan is supplying them with false gifts, empty monetary security and worldly success, then they assume they are being blessed by God. Cutting those things off that Satan would give them will allow the Holy Spirit to woo and draw them and reveal to them the need for His love.

Noah was responsible for the saving of his whole household because of his faithfulness. We, too, can take that position and see our loved ones delivered from the wickedness of this world. Abraham believed for his nephew, Lot, and before destruction came upon the wicked cities of Sodom and Gomorrah where he lived, the Lord sent His angels to bring Lot and his family out. The Lord will deliver His own who are following Him in holiness and righteousness. Only those who are unwilling to walk in the ways of the Lord and to depart from their sin and wickedness will suffer loss.

...the harvest is the end of the world (age); and the reapers are the angels. As therefore the tares are gathered and burned in the fire; so shall it be in the end of this world. The Son of man shall send forth his angels, and they shall gather out of his kingdom all things that offend, and them which do iniquity; And shall cast them into a furnace of fire: there shall be wailing and gnashing of teeth. Then shall the righteous shine forth as the sun in the kingdom of their Father. Who hath ears to hear, let him hear (Matthew 13:39-43). Immediately after the tribulation of those days...shall appear the sign

of the Son of man in heaven (Matthew 24:29-30). The righteous shall never be removed: but the wicked shall not inhabit the earth (Proverbs 10:30). For the upright shall dwell in the land, and the perfect shall remain in it. But the wicked shall be cut off from the earth, and the transgressors shall be rooted out of it (Proverbs 2:21-22).

Jesus Christ is coming again soon, and if we are to be caught up with Him at the end of this age, then we must be cleansed of all that offends Him.

Now this I say, brethren, that flesh and blood cannot inherit the kingdom of God; neither doth corruption inherit incorruption. Behold, I shew you a mystery; We shall not all sleep, but we shall all be changed, In a moment, in the twinkling of an eye, at the last trump: for the trumpet shall sound, and the dead shall be raised incorruptible, and we shall be changed. For this corruptible must put on incorruption, and this mortal must put on immortality (1 Corinthians 15:50-53). The resurrection that will occur at the end of this age and Christ's coming in glory is the hope of the church.

But I would not have you to be ignorant, brethren, concerning them which are asleep, that ye sorrow not, even as others which have no hope. For if we believe that Jesus died and rose again, even so them also which sleep in Jesus will God bring with him. For this we say unto you by the word of the Lord, that we which are alive and remain unto the coming of the Lord shall not prevent them which are asleep. For the Lord himself shall descend from heaven with a shout, with the voice of the archangel, and with the trump of God: and the dead in Christ shall rise first: Then we which are alive and remain shall be caught up together with them in the clouds, to meet the Lord in the air: and so shall we ever be with the Lord (1 Thessalonians 4:13-18). Christ's second coming shall be in glory and power. He shall come as the Lion of Judah. He came as the lamb of sacrifice at the first advent, but at the second advent, He shall appear as the Lion.

Reign of God's Kingdom

All Christians who have overcome shall rule and reign with Him when He sets up His kingdom on this earth. The saints who have died in times past, who have attained to the place of the overcomer shall, along with the overcomers of this hour, emerge as priests and kings to rule the earth for a thousand years with Christ. This thousand-year reign is known as the millenium. During this time the devil shall be chained and no wickedness or evil shall prevail. It will be an age of rest, glory and peace. The earth at last shall enjoy the blessings of God. There will be no more wars or sickness. All the earth shall walk in the knowledge of the Lord and be ruled and governed in His love and righteousness. God has beautiful plans for those who become overcomers; they shall sit on thrones with Him and be a part of His rulership.

And I saw thrones, and they sat upon them, and judgment was given unto them: and I saw the souls of them that were beheaded for the witness of Jesus, and for the word of God, and which had not worshipped the beast, neither his image, neither had received his mark upon their foreheads, or in their hands; and they lived and reigned with Christ a thousand years. But the rest of the dead lived not again until the thousand years were finished. This is the first resurrection. Blessed and holy is he that hath part in the first resurrection: on such the second death hath no power, but they shall be priests of God and of Christ, and shall reign with him a thousand years (Revelation 20:4-6). And they sung a new song, saying, Thou art worthy to take the book, and to open the seals thereof: for thou wast slain, and hast redeemed us to God by thy blood out of every kindred, and tongue, and people, and nation; And hast made us unto our God kings and priests: and we shall reign on the earth (Revelation 5:9-10). What a glorious inheritance!

Not only will mankind be blessed during the millenium, but

so will all of creation. All of the earth shall operate under the laws of God, and this is what shall bring heaven to earth at last.

The wolf also shall dwell with the lamb, and the leopard shall lie down with the kid; and the calf and the young lion and the fatling together; and a little child shall lead them. And the cow and the bear shall feed; their young ones shall lie down together: and the lion shall eat straw like the ox. And the sucking child shall play on the hole of the asp, and the weaned child shall put his hand on the cockatrice' den. They shall not hurt nor destroy in all my holy mountain: for the earth shall be full of the knowledge of the Lord, as the waters cover the sea (Isaiah 11:6-9).

All of the people of the earth shall enjoy this paradise for a thousand years; at the end of that time, the devil will be loosed for a little season and some will follow in his ways even after enjoying God's goodness.

Finally, the fire of God shall destroy them. Then the devil who deceived them shall be cast into the lake of fire forever. All of the dead who are not in Christ shall then be resurrected and will appear before the Great White Throne Judgment to be judged for their evil works. After this judgment they will be cast into the lake of fire which is the second death. They shall be tormented forever along with the devil and his demons. **And when the thousand years are expired, Satan shall be loosed out of his prison, And shall go out to deceive the nations which are in the four quarters of the earth, Gog and Magog, to gather them together to battle: the number of whom is as the sand of the sea. And they went up on the breadth of the earth, and compassed the camp of the saints about, and the beloved city: and fire came down from God out of heaven, and devoured them. And the devil that deceived them was cast into the lake of fire and brimstone, where the beast and the false prophet are, and shall be tormented day and night for ever and ever. And I saw a great white throne, and him that sat on it, from whose face the earth and the heaven fled away; and there** was found no place for them. And I saw the dead, small and great, stand before God; and the books were opened: and another book was opened, which is the book of life: and the dead were judged out of those things which were written in the books, according to their works. And the sea gave up the dead which were in it; and death and hell delivered up the dead which were in them: and they were judged every man according to their works. And death and hell were cast into the lake of fire. This is the second death. And whosoever was not found written in the book of life was cast into the lake of fire (Revelation 20:7-15).

After this God will create a new heaven and a new earth and make all things new for His people. They will have no more death, tears, sorrow, pain or crying.

The overcomers will inherit all things that have been promised them throughout the ages. The whole family of God will enjoy one another and God throughout eternity. Praise God!

And God shall wipe away all tears from their eyes; and there shall be no more death, neither sorrow, nor crying, neither shall there be any more pain: for the former things are passed away. And he that sat upon the throne said, Behold, I make all things new. And he said unto me, Write: for these words are true and faithful. And he said unto me, It is done. I am Alpha and Omega, the beginning and the end. I will give unto him that is athirst of the fountain of the water of life freely. He that overcometh shall inherit all things; and I will be his God, and he shall be my son (Revelation 21:4-7).

If we desire to be a son of God who inherits all things, then we must ask God to empower us with the Holy Spirit so that we can begin that walk today. We can be an overcomer through the power of THE CHRIST UNLIMITED. Jesus Christ led the way and we are to follow. **Hebrews 5:8-9 and 6:1** says **Though he were a Son, yet learned he obedience by the things which he suffered; And being made perfect, he became the author of eternal salvation unto all them that obey him...Therefore leav-**

ing the principles of the doctrine of Christ, let us go on unto perfection...

The Overcomer's Test

How does God test us? First, let's look at what the definition of a test is. Webster's dictionary says: (a) it is an examination or trial as to prove the value or ascertain the nature of something; (b) an event, set of circumstances, etc. that proves or tries a person's qualities (example: the delay was a test of his patience); (d) a set of questions or exercises, problems for determining a person's knowledge, abilities, aptitude, or qualification; an examination; (e) to refine (as gold); (f) to be rated as the result of a test. To condense this definition, a test then is a trial, proving and refining by an examination.

Psalm 26:2 says **Examine me, O Lord, and prove me; try my reins and my heart.** Then in **Jeremiah 17:10** we find the Lord saying, **I the Lord search the heart, I try the reins, even to give every man according to his ways, and according to the fruit of his doings.**

From these two Scriptures we see the Lord does test us to see what is in our hearts and then gives us the fruit or reward of that test. But the question is "How does God test us?" Does He use tragedies, sickness, terror and evil to test us, as so many people believe? No. We are tested by God similar to the way we take examinations in school. In school we have teachers who instruct us and books to study to gain knowledge so that when examination time comes, we are able to pass the tests. If we listen closely to our teacher and do our homework and studies well, then when the test comes we pass it. The more diligent we are as students, the better grades we make when test time comes. The same is true of our Christian walk. If we listen and obey our teacher (the Holy Spirit) and we study our testbook (the Bible), when the tests of life (trials and problems) come we shall overcome and pass the test. If, on the other hand, we are sitting at the feet of carnal T.V. and worldly friends and reading carnal books and magazines, when the tribulations of this life come, we fail the test. We end up with divorce, bankruptcy, fatal illnesses, loss of our children, etc. These things can be prevented or overcome if we learn God's way and obey Him.

How does God test us? By giving us choices. Our choices of yesterday have created the circumstances of today. If we do not choose to do the will of God, we are choosing our own way (which is the way of sin) and those choices are producing the problems in our lives. **Galatians 6:7-9** says **Be not deceived; God is not mocked: for whatsoever a man soweth, that shall he also reap. For he that soweth to his flesh shall of the flesh reap corruption; but he that soweth to the Spirit shall of the Spirit reap life everlasting. And let us not be weary in well doing; for in due season we shall reap, if we faint not.** We cannot blame others for our circumstances, even though they may be doing evil toward us, as evil can be overcome through the power of goodness in God. **Romans 12:19-21** says **Dearly beloved, avenge not yourselves, but rather give place unto wrath: for it is written, Vengeance is mine; I will repay, saith the Lord. Therefore if thine enemy hunger, feed him; if he thirst, give him drink: for in so doing thou shalt heap coals of fire on his head. Be not overcome of evil, but overcome evil with good.** Understanding the sowing and reaping principle, we must therefore begin to make the choices that agree with God's Word if we are to be victorious and pass our tests.

Psalm 26:2b says **...try my reins and my heart.** What does this mean? We bridle a horse to guide it; as we rein it, it will respond by obeying us if it is broken. If we are rebellious and refuse God's reins in our lives, we are like a wild, unbroken horse. A broken vessel before God is a vessel that has no rebellion in his heart but is totally submitted to the will of the Lord. When David cried out in **Psalm 51:17, The sacrifices of God are a broken spirit: a broken and a contrite heart, O God, thou wilt not**

despise, he was referring to the fact that those who have no re-bellion and are totally submitted are a sacrifice unto God.

Obedience is the test of our love for God. **John 14:15** says **If ye love me, keep my commandments.**

Let us take a little exam in some basic areas that God has commanded us to obey and see how we are scoring with God.

Test Responses -- (Use score box page 76)

Subject: Prayer

(1) "I personally spend a set time in prayer daily."

1 Thessalonians 5:17: Pray without ceasing.

(2) "As a family we pray and seek God together."

Ezra 8:21: Then I proclaimed a fast there, at the river of Ahava, that we might afflict ourselves before our God, to seek of Him a right way for us, and for our little ones, and for all our substance.

1 Peter 3:7: Likewise, ye husbands, dwell with them according to knowledge, giving honour unto the wife, as unto the weaker vessel, and as being heirs together of the grace of life; that your prayers be not hindered.

(3) "I join with others when corporate meetings are held in the church."

Luke 19:46a: (Jesus) Saying unto them, It is written, my house is the house of prayer...

Subject: The Word of God

(4) "I personally read and study the Word of God daily."

Proverbs 4:20-23: My son, attend to my words; incline thine ear unto my sayings. Let them not depart from thine eyes; keep them in the midst of thine heart. For they are life unto those that find them, and health to all their flesh. Keep thy heart with all diligence; for out of it are the issues of life.

(5) "I take advantage of the ministry of God's teachers and

attend Bible studies and read Spirit-anointed literature and listen to tapes when available."

2 Timothy 2:15: Study to shew thyself approved unto God, a workman that needeth not to be ashamed, rightly dividing the word of truth.

(6) "I share the Word of God with others as God has called me to be a witness to others daily."

Acts 5:42: And daily in the temple, and in every house, they ceased not to teach and preach Jesus Christ.

Subject: Relationships

(7) "I spend time with my family sharing in the Lord."

Deuteronomy 6:6-7: And these words, which I command thee this day, shall be in thine heart; And thou shalt teach them diligently unto thy children, and shalt talk of them when thou sittest in thine house, and when thou walkest by the way, and when thou liest down, and when thou risest up.

(8) "I spend time with my church family and like believers, developing relationships in Christ."

Hebrews 10:24-2: And let us consider one another to provoke unto love and to good works: Not forsaking the assembling of ourselves together, as the manner of some is; but exhorting one another: and so much the more, as ye see the day approaching.

(9) "I spend time developing my love relationship with the Lord by taking time to just be alone with Him."

Matthew 22:37: Jesus said unto him, Thou shalt love the Lord thy God with all thy heart, and with all thy soul, and with all thy mind.

Subject: Commitment to God

(10) "I am totally committed to do the perfect will of God."

Matthew 7:21: Not every one that saith unto me, Lord, Lord, shall enter into the kingdom of heaven; but he that doeth the will of my Father which is in heaven.

Test Number	A	B	C	D
Response:	Never	Seldom	Half of the time	Most of the time
1.				
2.				
3.				
4.				
5.				
6.				
7.				
8.				
9.				
10.				
Total check marks from each column	_____	_____	_____	_____
Score Points	A=0 pts.	B=3 pts. each	C =6 pts. each	D=10 pts. each
Total Points	_____	_____	_____	_____

TOTAL SCORE: _____

How does this test relate to how we walk with God? In **John 15:1-8** we are told to abide in Jesus and we will bear fruit. We are to bear fruit, more fruit, and much fruit. This parable, along with the parable of the sower and the seed in **Matthew 13** shows us our growth in Christ comes forth as the seed (the Word of God) is sown in our hearts. As we continue to nurture the Word, it produces fruit in our lives in different proportions: 30-fold, 60-fold, and 100-fold. The fruit of God is not only our good works, but the fruit of His Spirit listed in **Galatians 5:22-23: But the fruit of the Spirit is love, joy, peace, longsuffering, gentleness, goodness, faith, Meekness, temperance: against such there is no law.**

Thirty-fold Christians are a type of those spoken of in **1 Corinthians 3:1-3: And I, brethren, could not speak unto you as unto spiritual, but as unto carnal, even as unto babes in Christ. I have fed you with milk, and not with meat: for hitherto ye were not able to bear it, neither yet now are ye able. For ye are yet carnal: for whereas there is among you envying, and strife, and divisions, are ye not carnal, and walk as men?** Sixty-fold Christians go further in Christ but do not attain the ultimate goal of Christ being totally formed in them as do the hundred-fold Christians, the overcomers. Paul spoke of the prize of the high calling in God in Christ Jesus in **Philippians 3:14-15: I press toward the mark for the prize of the high calling of God in Christ Jesus. Let us therefore, as many as be perfect, be thus minded: and if in any thing ye be otherwise minded, God shall reveal even this unto you.** God desires that we all be overcomers and He tells us what the rewards for the overcomers are in **Revelation 2** and **3**. In **Revelation 21:7** He says, **He that overcometh shall inherit all things; and I will be his God, and he shall be my son.**

The Lord does not want us to remain babes or to be carnal or half-committed, but rather 100% committed to the will of God.

As you examine your score, you can see by the chart below where you are in your spiritual growth. The tabernacle plan is a type of Christian progression.

First, we come to the outer court for cleansing, then the inner court to light and bread (the Word), then the true priests of God enter into the holy of holies where there is communion with God at the mercy seat. Through Christ's death on the cross, the veil was rent between the inner court and the holy of holies so that we might enter into the place that once was reserved for only the Old Testament high priests.

Our Progression in Christ

30-Fold	60-Fold	100-Fold
New Birth	Growth in God	Fullness of God
Born Again	Sons of God	Born of God
Child	Servanthood	Fatherhood
Babe	Servant	Friend
Fruit	More Fruit	Much Fruit (John 15)
Called	Chosen	Faithful (Rev. 17:14)
Blade	Ear	Full Corn (Mk. 4:28)
Corn	Wine	Oil (Deut. 11:14)
Babes	Servants	Heirs (Gal. 4)
Justified	Sanctified	Glorified (Rom. 8)
Passover	Pentecost	Tabernacles
Egypt	Wilderness	Promised Land
Baptized in Water	Baptized in Holy Spirit	Baptized in Fire
Outer Court	Inner Court	Holy of Holies

From this chart we see the first column represents our entry into God, the second our growth in God and the last our becoming overcomers in God.

This little test will give you an idea of your present commitment to God. You can see which range you are in by your score. If you scored around 60 you are growing in God, if only around 30 you are still a babe or a carnal Christian. Those approaching 100 are pressing into the overcomer's walk. Those who score below 30 need to seriously examine their walk with God. They are either totally backslidden or possibly not even saved.

This test, of course, is not foolproof as only God sees our hearts; we could score 100% and still fail the test if our motives are wrong. We must also realize that complete obedience, if done only by our efforts or works, is still failing as there is only one way to overcoming self and sin and that is through Jesus' death on the cross and our faith in what He's done for us. Works alone are not sufficient; however, our works and our actions reveal what is in our hearts. **(Proverbs 20:11** says, **Even a child is known by his doings, whether his work be pure, and whether it be right.)**

This test is meant only to inspire you to become an overcomer and to show you any areas in your life that could cause you to fall short of that goal. Let us press into God more so that we can receive the prize of the high calling of an overcomer!

Index

Additional Books by the Author:

Book Titles in the OVERCOMING LIFE SERIES:

PROVE ALL THINGS
THE TRUE GOD
THE WILL OF GOD
KEYS TO THE KINGDOM
EXPOSING SATAN'S DEVICES
HEALING OF THE SPIRIT, SOUL & BODY
NEITHER MALE NOR FEMALE
EXTREMES OR BALANCE?
THE PATHWAY INTO THE OVERCOMER'S WALK

Book Titles in the END TIMES SERIES:

MARK OF GOD OR MARK OF THE BEAST
PERSONAL SPIRITUAL WARFARE

Christ Unlimited Ministries, Inc.
P.O. Box 850
Dewey, AZ 86327
U.S.A.
For online orders, please visit our website:
http://www.BibleResources.org

Postnote

The Millers are very glad to receive mail from their readers; however, they are unable to answer the letters personally due the volume of mail that they receive. They will be happy to pray along with their intercessors for all who write with a prayer request; although they do no outside counseling as they believe this should be directed to local pastors as outlined in Scripture.

Christ Unlimited Ministries, Inc. is a non-profit church 501(c) (3) corporation. All contributions are tax deductible. We appreciate your prayers, encouragement and support. Your purchase of this book makes it possible for us to share free copies of Bibles, teaching literature, tracts and downloadable audio/video materials with ministers in third world countries who would otherwise not be able to purchase them.

The Lord gave the word: great was the company of those that published it (Psalm 68:11).

For Additional Study

This book is taken from a course of Bible studies called the Overcoming Life Series. The entire series is a virtual "spiritual tool chest," as it covers a multitude of subjects every Christian faces in his walk with God. It also answers questions that many believers have concerning the current move of God. These are dealt with in a balanced approach and in the light of the Scripture. God's people are not to live frustrated, defeated lives, but rather they are to be victorious overcomers! Other books available with their companion workbooks are:

PROVE ALL THINGS - Christ warned that great deception would be one of the signs of the end times. In this book, instruction is given on how to recognize false prophets and teachings. Clear Scriptural guidelines are given on discerning the Spirit of truth versus the spirit of error. The book deals with how to judge without being judgmental.

THE TRUE GOD - This is a teaching on the character of God, explaining why God does certain things, and why it is against His nature to do other things. It differentiates between the things for which God is responsible and the things for which the devil is responsible. Our responsibility as Christians destined to overcome is made clear so that we can live victorious lives.

THE WILL OF GOD - This lesson teaches us not only how to know the will of God in our personal lives, family, ministry and finances, but also brings understanding as to why God allows sin, sickness and suffering in the world. As overcomers, Christians are not to suffer under many of the things we have accepted as normal.

KEYS TO THE KINGDOM - Instruction on how to gain authority in God's Kingdom through prayer is the topic of this book. Many principles and methods of prayer are covered, such as pray ing in the Spirit, fasting and prayer, travailing prayer, praise, intercession and spiritual warfare.

EXPOSING SATAN'S DEVICES - This book is a powerful expose' of Satan's tricks, tactics and lies. Cult and Occultic methods and groups are listed so Christians can detect their activity. Demon activity is discussed and deliverance and casting out demons is dealt with in detail. Satan's kingdom is uncovered and the Christian is taught to overcome through spiritual discernment and warfare.

HEALING OF THE SPIRIT, SOUL AND BODY - This book teaches how to overcome emotional problems, as well as physical ones, and how to receive divine healing. It also teaches how to renew the carnal mind and walk in the spirit of life, thereby overcoming depression, loneliness and fear.

NEITHER MALE NOR FEMALE - What is the woman's role in the church and home? Who is a woman's spiritual head and covering? Does God call women to the five-fold ministry? What does God's Word say about divorce, celibacy and choosing a marriage partner? These and other woman related topics are Scripturally examined.

EXTREMES OR BALANCE? - Many Christians have hurt the cause of Christ through "out-of-balance" teachings and demonstrations. This book shows how to avoid those areas. It also deals wisely with the excesses and extremes in the body of Christ.

THE PATHWAY INTO THE OVERCOMER'S WALK - This book contains answers to the questions an overcomer faces as he presses toward the prize of the high calling in Christ Jesus. How can we be conformed to the image of Christ? How does the Holy Spirit work with the overcomers in the end times? What are the overcomer's rewards?

PERSONAL SPIRITUAL WARFARE - Explains the invisible world of spiritual forces that influence our lives and how good can prevail over the evil around us as we prepare for the new kingdom age that is coming. This book will help you overcome problems in your finances, marriage, the emotional pressures of fear, anger and hurt. Here are the keys to victory through spiritual warfare.

MARK OF GOD OR MARK OF THE BEAST - Much has been written and said about the mark of the beast, but little has been said about the mark of God. What does the 666 mean and what is this mysterious mark? How is it linked to the world of finance? Has this mark already begun? This book answers many questions about the mark of the beast and the mark of God, and how they affect Christians.

Please visit our website for information on how to order the complete "Overcoming Life Bible Study Series."

www.BibleResources.org

Purpose and Vision

Go ye therefore, and teach all nations, baptiz-
ing them in the name of the Father, and of the Son,
and of the Holy Ghost: Teaching them to observe
all things whatsoever I have commanded you: and,
lo, I am with you alway, even unto the end of the
world. Amen.

Matthew 28:19,20

Christ Unlimited is not "another denomination," sect, or just
a separate group. It is an arm of the Body of Christ — the Church
of Jesus Christ, which has been called to strengthen the Body at
large. We also believe we have been called to help establish the
Kingdom of God in the earth.

Christ Unlimited is involved with all Bible-believing Christians regardless of their church or denominational affiliations and
committed to helping wherever possible in evangelistic and teaching outreaches.

Christ Unlimited believes that time is running out and the
Gospel has not been preached to every creature. Many nations
have not heard the Gospel, and in many places, doors for evange-
lism are closing. We believe it is time all Christians cooperated
with the Lord in breaking down denominational walls for a united
front line against the kingdom of darkness and in setting up the
Kingdom of the Lord Jesus Christ by the power of the Holy Spirit.

Christ Unlimited provides such tools as to enable the saints
of God to establish the Kingdom of God in the earth. We encourage groups of prayer warriors who will pray, fast, and intercede
for the nations. This, we believe, is weapon number one. We teach
believers how to overcome through spiritual warfare and through

knowing how to use their authority in Christ Jesus through the Word and the power of the Holy Spirit.

Christians need to know how to bring down the forces of darkness in their own lives and in the lives of those to whom they minister. We provide such tools as Bibles, literature, Christ Unlimited books, and an online prayer ministry. We publish the Gospel going out via any means of communication, including the Internet, videos, as well as literature. We have teaching seminars, Bible schools, and correspondence courses, all aimed at winning souls to Christ and building the Body of Christ into maturity.

Bud and Betty Miller serve the Lord together as founders of the multi-visioned ministry outreach, Christ Unlimited. The outreaches of this ministry have stemmed from a tremendous desire to see the Word of God taught in its balanced entirety. The Millers are firm believers in prayer and, through prayer, have seen many released from the bondages of fear, failure, and defeat.

The outreaches of Christ Unlimited are in obedience to the words of our Lord in **Mark 16:15**: **Go ye into all the world and preach the gospel to every creature.** This mandate from the Lord presents a challenge to our generation as an estimated 25 percent of the world's population still have not heard the Good News of Jesus Christ.

Christ Unlimited Ministries also is dedicated to teaching God's Word. **Hosea 4:6** says: **My people are destroyed for lack of knowledge.** Many Christians are leading defeated lives simply because they do not know God's Word in its fullest.

Christ Unlimited Ministries has provided for those who desire to know God's Word in a greater way. The main thrust of the teaching and literature is directed at "How to be an overcomer." In the endtimes, we must be prepared to overcome the onslaughts of Satan. Many Christians are suffering needlessly, because they do not know how to overcome sickness, depression, divorce, fear, and financial failure. Christ Unlimited Ministries provides answers for troubled families as well as trains workers for service.

www.ingramcontent.com/pod-product-compliance
Lightning Source LLC
Chambersburg PA
CBHW020950030426
42339CB00004B/31